Seasoned to Taste

SAVORING THE SCENIC CITY
WITH THE JUNIOR LEAGUE OF CHATTANOOGA

Seasoned to Taste

SAVORING THE SCENIC CITY

Copyright © 2011 by
Junior League of Chattanooga
622 East 4th Street
Chattanooga, Tennessee 37403
423-267-5053

Photography © as noted on page 189
constitutes an extension of this copyright page

Published by

||| Favorite Recipes® Press

An imprint of

FRP®INC

A wholly owned subsidiary of Southwestern
P.O. Box 305142
Nashville, Tennessee 37230
800-358-0560

Editorial Director: Mary Cummings
Art Director and Book Design: Steve Newman
Project Editor: Tanis Westbrook

Library of Congress Control Number: 2010937612
ISBN: 978-0-9611806-1-4

This cookbook is a collection of favorite recipes,
which are not necessarily original recipes.

Manufactured in the United States of America
First Printing: 2011
12,500 copies

Foreword

For more than ninety years now, the Junior League of Chattanooga has had a profound effect on this great city, touching and transforming the lives of so many of its citizens. Born and raised in Chattanooga in the 1930s, I saw the value of a volunteer and wanted to be part of such a high-caliber group of hard-working, committed, and forward-thinking women. And so it began for me in the 1950s, when I joined the League and formed a strong relationship that has lasted ever since. It is an honor to be a part of the League and it is with great pleasure that I write this foreword for the new cookbook, *Seasoned to Taste: Savoring the Scenic City*. That's exactly what the title of this book reminds us to do: savor life and our hometown through the fruits of our labor, whether that be through the tradition of cooking or by donating our time and efforts to our city through voluntarism.

I feel fully qualified to talk about the importance of cooking because at age 84 I have had time to accumulate over 100 cookbooks, including our League's first book, *Dinner on the Diner*. Each one has helped me feed a growing family of a husband and four sons along with their wives and children, and later on, members of the Medical Society committees, the McCallie School, and the First Presbyterian Church. My memory takes me back to my early days of cooking, done on a wood-burning stove using all sorts of gadgets cranked by hand. My, how times have changed! The bustling activity in the kitchen surrounding the art of cooking is timeless though, and can create traditions that last a lifetime.

As an Emeritus League member, I am delighted to see a new generation of women who know that a well-prepared meal is the glue that holds family and friends together. So I say with all my heart, get on with the work of making meals and memories using new techniques and new foods for a hungry and deserving new generation. Those you love and care for appreciate you, as does our Scenic City!

Maddin Lupton McCallie
Sustainer Emeritus
Junior League of Chattanooga

Mrs. Maddin Lupton McCallie (1926–2010) was a dedicated member of the Junior League of Chattanooga for sixty-one years. We are grateful for her many years of selfless leadership and service to our community.

Acknowledgments

The Junior League of Chattanooga would like to express their gratitude to the
following organizations for their generous contributions toward the development of this project.
Your support in this collaborative effort ensures a legacy of continued positive community impact.

PRESENTING SPONSOR

Children's Hospital at Erlanger

SUPPORTING SPONSORS

BB&T—Huffaker & Trimble

Baker, Donelson, Bearman, Caldwell & Berkowitz, PC

Berke, Berke & Berke, Attorneys at Law

Chambliss, Bahner & Stophel, PC

Gigi's Cupcakes

Hunt Nissan of Chattanooga

Husch Blackwell, LLP

Miller & Martin, PLLC

Tennessee Valley Authority

MaryMargaret Chambliss, Photography

Jane Chambliss Drennen, Food Stylist

MaryMargaret Chambliss is an event, wedding, and food photographer based in Birmingham,
Alabama. Her work has appeared most recently in *Southern Living* magazine. She and her sister,
Jane, inherited their mother's love of photography and cooking, respectively, and they enjoy
the opportunity to collaborate creatively on concepts and projects. Jane's work has been featured
in *Southern Living*, *Cooking Light*, *Paula Deen*, and *Sandra Lee* magazines.

Additional photos provided by Vincent Rizzo and Warren-McLelland Aerial Photography

Dedication

This cookbook is dedicated to those who taught us to savor every bite life has to offer.
We hope our book stirs up fond memories of experiences in the kitchen, and that the recipes in
this collection create new traditions for you, your family, and your friends for years to come.

Claudette Anderson . . . . mother of Donna Brody

Martha Kemp Barber . . . . grandmother of Hillary Barber

Mary Drew Beard . . . . daughter of Molly Beard

Emma Virginia Birnbaum . . . . daughter of Ginger Birnbaum

Ginger Birnbaum . . . . friend of the Recipe Committee Members

George Brinkley . . . . father of Rebecca Brinkley

Nell Brinkley . . . . mother of Rebecca Brinkley

Lauren Nikole Brockman . . . . granddaughter of Sara Fields

Vivian Meade Brockman . . . . granddaughter of Sara Fields

Grace Brody . . . . daughter of Donna Brody

Greer Brody . . . . son of Donna Brody

Griffin Brody . . . . son of Donna Brody

Kirk Brody . . . . husband of Donna Brody

Glenn William Brown, Junior . . . . husband of Marilyn Voges Brown

Phyllis Byrum . . . . mother of Meredith Byrum Brown

Allen Clark . . . . husband of Shannon Clark

Maeve Clark . . . . daughter of Shannon Clark

Spencer Clark . . . . son of Shannon Clark

Coughlin Cooper . . . . friend of Donna Brody

Susan Critchfield . . . . mother-in-law of Theresa Critchfield

Jay Elliott . . . . husband of Missy Elliott

Pamela Robinson Farless . . . . mother of Ashley Farless

Nina Fazio . . . . mother of Christy Fazio

Charolyn Ferguson . . . . mother of Cynthia Fagan

Harry L. Fields, III . . . . husband of Sara Fields

Elva Hill . . . . grandmother of Heather H. Sveadas

Cheryl Ann Imami . . . . mother of Jasmin Nora Rippon

Elizabeth Ingram . . . . mother of Laura Ketcham

Virginia Suzanne King . . . . mother of Ginger Birnbaum

Jackie Kirtley . . . . mother of Kacy Lemm

Peggy Leach . . . . mother of Andee Guthrie

Julia Platt Leonard . . . . daughter of Anne H. Platt

Debbie Light . . . . mother of Theresa Critchfield

Dr. Laura Farless MacGregor . . . . sister of Ashley Farless

Brooks McKenna . . . . son of Missy McKenna

Sarah McKenzie . . . . mother of Beth McKenzie

Judy Nichols . . . . mother of Amy Jackson

Suzanne King Nolan . . . . mother of Chrissy Nolan

Leigh Pleva . . . . daughter of Susan Pleva

Debbie Massari Red . . . . mother of Sara Page Red-Barnwell

Maddin Nora Rippon . . . . daughter of Jasmin Nora Rippon

Ryan Rose . . . . husband of Billie Rose

Sonja Meyer Shamblin . . . . mother of Katie Shamblin Wilson

Betty Thomas Smith . . . . mother of Angela Ballard

M. Ruth Thomas . . . . mother of Tahnika N. Rodriguez

Jane Weathers . . . . mother of Jill Glenn

Chad Wolford . . . . husband of Lindsay Wolford

Finally, we dedicate this cookbook to our wonderful community.
You continue to motivate us to do more and are the inspiration for this labor of love.

Junior League of Chattanooga

As the second oldest Junior League in the South, we strive to make positive changes in our community. Dating back to 1917, our League has partnered with local hospitals to operate baby clinics and nutrition centers and has provided clothing and comfort to displaced children. We have established reading programs and distributed scholarship funds to local schools and special educational centers. Through projects and financial support, our League strives to improve the health of children and the future of families in our beloved city.

We are proud to serve and be a part of such an exceptional community, and we look forward to continuing the tradition for years to come. Through the purchase of *Seasoned to Taste: Savoring the Scenic City*, your contribution will help us continue our efforts. Ninety-four percent of every dollar we generate supports our mission to develop the potential of women and improve the community through the effective action and leadership of trained volunteers. The Junior League of Chattanooga is committed to the continuous improvement and transformation of this already great city, and we thank you for your support.

MISSION STATEMENT

Junior League of Chattanooga, Inc., is an organization of
women committed to promoting voluntarism, developing the
potential of women, and improving communities through
the effective action and leadership of trained volunteers.
Its purpose is exclusively educational and charitable.

VISION STATEMENT

The Junior League of Chattanooga:
Women as Catalysts for Lasting Community Change

Junior League of Chattanooga, Inc., reaches out to women of all
races, religions, and national origins who demonstrate
an interest and a commitment to voluntarism. The JLC has more
than 600 active and sustaining members. The JLC is a
member of the Association of Junior Leagues International, a coalition
of 296 Junior League organizations in 4 countries.

Introduction

There's a popular saying that goes, "I wasn't born in the South, but I got here as quick as I could!" The same can be said about Chattanooga—with its genuine Southern hospitality and charm, a melting pot of locals and transplants are thrilled to call it home.

On cross-country road trips as a child, I was fascinated with the city. Before beginning any journey, I would firmly implore my parents to "wake me when we get to Chattanooga!" lest I accidentally nap through the experience. The region is irresistible: looming, lush mountains; sparkling lakes and winding rivers; and, as you crest the ridge headed to downtown, the sweeping vista of the city leaves you breathless.

Chattanooga is nicknamed the Scenic City, and with good reason. The changing landscapes and activities present residents and visitors alike the chance to fall in love with the area each season. This was the inspiration for *Seasoned to Taste*. For spring, summer, autumn, and winter, you will find fabulous recipes that reflect the ingredients and traditions of the season paired with unique local events and scenery to be enjoyed during that special time of year.

Owners of Junior League cookbooks expect to find a treasure trove of splendid dishes, and our book is no exception. Our volunteers have spent countless hours testing, tasting, and selecting the community's finest recipes that appear on these pages. Like our community, the Junior League of Chattanooga blends history and traditions with a vision for the future. The publishing of *Seasoned to Taste* exemplifies all aspects of our mission: developing the potential of women, improving our community, and promoting voluntarism.

Proceeds from this book will propel us forward into the next generation of new and strengthened community partnerships, progressive needs-based projects, and innovative outreach programs.

Seasoned to Taste is a valentine to our beloved city. It is our hope that we have captured the essence of what we admire, appreciate, and celebrate in our kitchens and our lives.

We invite you to join us in Savoring the Scenic City, and we thank you for helping us continue to make an impact in our community!

Warmest wishes,

Billie Rose
Cookbook Chair
Junior League of Chattanooga

Seasoned to Taste

Contents

Denotes second helpings
from
Dinner on the Diner

A Season of Renewal

It's time to open the windows and breathe in fresh air. Listen for the mimicking sounds of Tennessee mockingbirds to fill moonlit nights, for their enjoyable songs herald the much-anticipated arrival of spring! The unfolding of majestic purple irises and the bursting of chartreuse flowers on the tulip poplars add to the dazzling landscape sweeping across the mountains and valleys surrounding Chattanooga.

Down south, we emerge from our post-winter lull to gather together for a drink on the porch while the little ones chase butterflies or take off down the street on dusty bikes. Gardens are planted and tended, local markets open with asparagus and tender greens, art and food festivals abound, and the region is alive with a rejuvenated energy.

As the days grow longer, homes are brightened from the added sunlight and refreshed from the completion of spring-cleaning chores and projects. Passover and Easter are special times celebrated with family and friends. Egg hunts abound in Chattanooga—be sure to get your basket over to Coolidge Park, where more than 50,000 eggs await gleeful, treasure-seeking children.

Spring defines the emergence of the Scenic City's local food resources as access to farm fresh food becomes bountiful. Through shareholding on farms, community and school gardens, and memberships to receive weekly produce boxes, Chattanooga dedication to community-supported agriculture continues to ripen. From the beginning of the season, a farmers' market can be found within the city most days of the week.

Spring

Spring

Supper in the Garden

Basil Mojitos
Legacy Tea
Bleu Camembert Torta
Pan-Seared Tarragon Chicken
Spring Peas
Best Biscuits
Jam Cake
Six-Flavor Pound Cake

ARTICHOKE MELBAS

SERVES 6 TO 8

1 (14-ounce) can artichoke hearts, drained
1 cup (4 ounces) grated Parmesan cheese
3/4 cup mayonnaise
2 tablespoons sherry
1/2 teaspoon garlic powder
Melba toasts

Cut each artichoke heart into thirds. Combine the cheese, mayonnaise, sherry and garlic powder in a bowl and mix well. Place an artichoke heart third on each Melba toast and place on a baking sheet. Cover each with a spoonful of the cheese mixture. Broil under a preheated broiler until light brown.

BLEU CHEESE BACON PUFFS

SERVES 8 TO 10

1 1/2 cups water
1/2 cup (1 stick) butter
1 1/2 cups all-purpose flour
1/2 teaspoon kosher salt
1/4 teaspoon freshly ground black pepper
1/4 teaspoon cayenne pepper
6 eggs
8 ounces crumbled bleu cheese
8 slices bacon, crisp-cooked and crumbled
1/4 cup finely chopped chives

Bring the water and butter to a boil in a saucepan. Remove from the heat and cool for 30 seconds. Add the flour, kosher salt, black pepper and cayenne pepper. Cook over medium-high heat until the mixture forms a smooth ball, beating constantly with a wooden spoon. Remove from the heat and place in a mixing bowl. Cool for 4 to 5 minutes. Add the eggs one at a time, beating well after each addition. Beat in the cheese, bacon and chives. Drop the dough by rounded teaspoonfuls 2 inches apart onto a lightly greased baking sheet. Bake in a preheated 400-degree oven for 20 to 25 minutes or until golden brown. Serve warm or at room temperature.

NOTE: The dough may be spooned into a pastry bag or a sealable plastic bag with the corner removed and piped onto a baking sheet.

These can be made ahead, chilled, and reheated gently in the oven before serving.

The base of this recipe is a basic pâte à choux—a light dough used for cream puffs, profiteroles, éclairs, and other sweet treats. Instead of a leavening agent, it's the steam from the heat of the oven which makes the dough rise, creating the puffed result.

This recipe can have many variations—just swap out the savory ingredients (pepper, cheese, bacon, and chives) with your favorites. Or, omit them altogether and fill the baked puffs with whipped cream for a tasty dessert.

TOPPLIN' TOMATOES

MAKES 30 TO 35

1 cup mayonnaise
3/4 cup plus 1 tablespoon freshly grated
    Parmesan cheese
8 ounces cream cheese, softened
1 cup cottage cheese
5 tablespoons minced parsley
2 tablespoons Worcestershire sauce

1/2 teaspoon kosher salt
2 pounds bacon, crisp-cooked
    and crumbled
30 to 35 small to medium unbruised
    Campari tomatoes
Kosher salt

Combine the mayonnaise, Parmesan cheese, cream cheese, cottage cheese, parsley, Worcestershire sauce and 1/2 teaspoon kosher salt in a bowl and mix well. Stir in the bacon. Chill in the refrigerator.

Cut a small slice off the bottom of each tomato to enable the tomatoes to stand upright. Cut a small slice off the top of each tomato and scoop out the tomatoes with the small end of a melon baller. Sprinkle lightly with additional kosher salt. Let stand to drain. Spoon the cheese mixture into each tomato using the melon baller. Chill for up to 1 hour. Serve skewered for easy handling.

CRAB-STUFFED MUSHROOMS

SERVES 30

16 ounces cream cheese, softened
8 ounces fresh or frozen crab meat,
    shells removed and meat flaked
1/2 cup (2 ounces) grated Parmesan cheese
    or asiago cheese
1/4 cup olive oil
1/2 cup lemon juice
1/4 cup chopped parsley

1/3 cup bread crumbs
2 tablespoons minced shallots
1/4 cup Cognac
1/2 tablespoon Dijon mustard
1/4 cup all-purpose flour
1/2 tablespoon salt
1 teaspoon pepper
30 mushrooms

Mix the cream cheese, crab meat, Parmesan cheese, olive oil, lemon juice, parsley, bread crumbs, shallots, Cognac, Dijon mustard, flour, salt and pepper in a bowl. Remove the stems from the mushrooms. Stuff the mushroom caps with the crab meat mixture and place on a greased baking sheet. Bake in a preheated 375-degree oven until light brown. Serve immediately.

Photograph for this recipe appears on page 29.

Never soak mushrooms. Rinse them quickly and then pat dry with paper towels.

BLEU CAMEMBERT TORTA

SERVES 20 TO 25

8 ounces cream cheese, softened
2 tablespoons milk
1 cup pecans, toasted and chopped
16 ounces cream cheese, softened
4 ounces Camembert cheese
4 ounces bleu cheese
4 ounces Swiss cheese, finely shredded

Line an 8-inch pie plate with plastic wrap, leaving enough to hang over the side. Mix 8 ounces cream cheese and the milk in a bowl with a fork until smooth. Spread in the lined pie plate. Sprinkle with the pecans and press to adhere. Chill in the refrigerator.

Combine 16 ounces cream cheese, the Camembert cheese, bleu cheese and Swiss cheese in a mixing bowl and beat until blended. Spoon over the pecan layer. Spread to the edge of the pie plate and press down. Chill for 4 hours. Invert onto a serving platter and remove the plastic wrap. Serve with firm crackers.

GARLIC AND DILL FETA CHEESE SPREAD

SERVES 10 TO 12

8 ounces cream cheese, softened
4 ounces feta cheese, crumbled
1/4 cup mayonnaise
1 garlic clove, minced
1 tablespoon chopped fresh dill weed, or 1/2 teaspoon dried dill weed
1/2 teaspoon seasoned pepper
1/4 teaspoon salt

Process the cream cheese, feta cheese, mayonnaise, garlic, dill weed, pepper and salt in a food processor until smooth. Spoon into a bowl. Chill, covered, for 8 hours. Serve on cucumber slices drizzled with olive oil, or use as a spread for bagels, sandwiches or crackers.

After handling fresh garlic, rub your hands and fingers on stainless steel to remove the lingering odor.

HEIRLOOM SALSA VERDE

SERVES 10

5 or 6 tomatillos
Sea salt to taste
2 or 3 heirloom tomatoes
Juice of 1 lime
1/4 cup coarsely chopped cilantro leaves
1/2 tablespoon kosher salt

Cut the tomatillos into halves. Sprinkle sea salt on the cut sides. Place cut side down on a foil-lined baking sheet. Broil in a preheated broiler on high for 10 to 15 minutes or until the tomatillos are wrinkled and light brown, watching carefully to prevent overbrowning. Remove from the oven to cool. Pull off the skins from the tomatillos. Core the tomatoes. Remove the meat, reserving the shells for another purpose. Mix the tomato meat, tomatillos, lime juice, cilantro and kosher salt in a bowl, pulling apart the pulp if needed.

NOTE: Serve with chips or as an accompaniment to meat dishes or tacos.

BASIL MOJITOS

SERVES 1

2 sprigs of fresh mint, chopped
2 sprigs of fresh basil, chopped
1 tablespoon sugar
3 tablespoons fresh lime juice
1 1/2 ounces light rum
Chilled club soda or seltzer water
Fresh mint, fresh basil leaves and lime slices for garnish

Crush the chopped mint and chopped basil with the sugar and lime juice with the back of a spoon in a tall glass until the sugar is dissolved. Stir in the rum. Add ice cubes. Add enough club soda to fill the glass and stir well. Garnish with mint, basil and lime.

WEDDING BELL PUNCH

SERVES 24 TO 30

1 quart Mayfield vanilla ice cream, softened
1 quart Mayfield pineapple sherbet, softened
1/2 gallon (8 cups) Mayfield orange juice, chilled
1/2 gallon (8 cups) Mayfield lemonade, chilled

Combine the ice cream, sherbet, orange juice and lemonade in a punch bowl and mix well. Ladle into punch cups.

LEMON DROP PUNCH

SERVES 12

3 lemons, at room temperature
1/2 cup sugar
1/2 cup water
1 (750-milliliter) bottle dry Champagne, chilled
1 cup vodka, chilled
1 lemon, thinly sliced for garnish

Squeeze the juice from three lemons through a strainer to remove the pulp. You should have a minimum of 1/4 cup juice. Heat the sugar and water in a small saucepan over medium-high heat, stirring until the sugar dissolves. Bring to a boil; remove from the heat. Let stand for 2 hours to cool. Chill for 2 hours longer. Combine the Champagne, vodka, lemon juice and chilled sugar syrup in a punch bowl and stir to blend well. Garnish with the lemon slices. Serve in Champagne flutes.

> *For maximum juice from lemons and limes, microwave about fifteen seconds before juicing.*

LEGACY TEA

SERVES 12 TO 15

4 extra-large family-size tea bags
1 gallon (16 cups) hot water
2²/3 cups sugar
1 cup lemon juice
1¹/2 cups orange juice
1 (1-liter) bottle ginger ale
Sprigs of fresh mint for garnish

Place the tea bags in the hot water in a large stockpot. Cover and steep. Remove the tea bags. Add the sugar, lemon juice, orange juice and ginger ale and mix well. Pour into clean jugs and chill. Garnish with mint.

Photograph for this recipe appears on page 29.

Photograph for this recipe appears on page 29.

CRAB QUICHE

SERVES 8 TO 16

2 unbaked (9-inch) pie shells
2 tablespoons minced green onions
1 tablespoon butter or margarine, melted
4 eggs, beaten
1¹/2 cups heavy whipping cream, whipped
1 pound fresh or frozen crab meat, shells removed and meat flaked
1 cup (4 ounces) shredded Swiss cheese
2 tablespoons sherry
3/4 teaspoon salt
¹/8 teaspoon ground red pepper
1 sprig of fresh parsley for garnish

Bake the pie shells in a preheated 400-degree oven for 3 minutes. Prick the bottoms and sides with a fork. Bake for 5 minutes longer. Increase the oven temperature to 425 degrees. Sauté the green onions in the butter in a large skillet. Add the eggs and whipped cream. Stir in the crab meat, cheese, sherry, salt and red pepper. Pour into the prebaked pie shells. Bake for 15 minutes. Reduce the oven temperature to 325 degrees. Bake for 25 to 30 minutes longer or until set. Let stand for 10 minutes before serving.

SISI'S STICKY BUNS

MAKES 2¹/2 DOZEN

1 cup milk
5 tablespoons granulated sugar
1 teaspoon salt
1/4 cup shortening
1 envelope dry yeast
1 tablespoon granulated sugar
2 tablespoons lukewarm water
1 egg, beaten
4 cups all-purpose flour, sifted
Pecans to taste
1/2 cup (1 stick) unsalted butter, softened
1 cup plus 2 tablespoons packed brown sugar (8 ounces)
Cinnamon to taste
Raisins to taste

Heat the milk in a saucepan over medium-high heat for 5 minutes. Reduce the heat to low. Stir in 5 tablespoons granulated sugar, the salt and shortening. Remove from the heat and cool briefly. Dissolve the yeast and 1 tablespoon granulated sugar in the lukewarm water in a bowl. Add to the milk mixture and mix well. Beat in the egg and as much of the flour as possible without kneading. Beat in as much of the remaining flour as possible by hand. Place on a lightly floured surface. Knead in enough of the remaining flour until the dough is no longer sticky. Place in a greased bowl, turning to coat the surface. Let rise for 4 hours or until doubled in bulk.

Sprinkle pecans in well-greased baking pans. Cream the butter and brown sugar in a mixing bowl until light and fluffy. Roll the dough 1/4 inch thick on a lightly floured surface. Spread with the brown sugar mixture. Sprinkle with cinnamon and raisins. Roll up as for a jelly roll. Cut into 1/2- to 3/4-inch slices. Place in the prepared baking pans. Let rise for 1 hour. Bake in a preheated 350-degree oven for 25 minutes or until brown. Cool in the pans for 5 minutes. Invert onto a serving platter.

BLUEBERRY COFFEE CAKE

SERVES 9

3/4 cup sugar
1/4 cup (1/2 stick) salted butter, softened
1/2 cup mayonnaise
1/2 cup milk
2 cups all-purpose flour
2 teaspoons baking powder

1/2 teaspoon salt
1 1/2 cups fresh or frozen blueberries
1/2 cup sugar
1/3 cup all-purpose flour
1/2 teaspoon cinnamon
1/4 cup (1/2 stick) salted butter, melted

Cream 3/4 cup sugar, 1/4 cup butter and the mayonnaise in a mixing bowl until light and fluffy. Stir in the milk, 2 cups flour, the baking powder and salt. Fold in the blueberries. Pour into an 8×8-inch baking pan. Mix 1/2 cup sugar, 1/3 cup flour, the cinnamon and 1/4 cup melted butter in a bowl until crumbly. Sprinkle over the batter. Bake in a preheated 375-degree oven for 55 minutes or until brown. Serve warm.

BEST BISCUITS

SERVES 6 TO 8

1 tablespoon corn oil
2 cups buttermilk
1/3 cup corn oil
4 cups (about) White Lily Self-Rising Flour
1/4 cup (1/2 stick) unsalted butter, melted

Coat a cast-iron skillet thoroughly with 1 tablespoon corn oil. Mix the buttermilk and 1/3 cup corn oil in a bowl. Stir in 3 1/2 cups of the flour. Place on a lightly floured surface and knead slightly, folding the edges toward the middle and adding enough of the remaining flour as needed until the dough is no longer sticky. Turn the dough and pat into a very thick circle. Cut with a floured biscuit cutter. Arrange in the prepared skillet. Bake in a preheated 450-degree oven for 15 to 20 minutes or until golden brown. Remove from the oven. Brush with the melted butter before serving.

Photograph for this recipe appears on page 15.

Growing up in our family, we never paid attention when our mothers, grandmothers, and aunts made biscuits—it was just the expected foundation to any southern meal. When we grew up and flew the nest, the siblings and cousins in my generation realized we were missing that special biscuit-making skill, and thus, our meals weren't turning out nearly as well in our own homes. We each separately returned to my mother for biscuit tutorials, as the recipe was never written down through the generations... until now. It's about time!

GRAPE SALAD

SERVES *12* TO *15*

4 pounds green grapes and red grapes
8 ounces cream cheese, softened
1 cup sour cream
1/2 cup granulated sugar
1 teaspoon vanilla extract
1 cup chopped pecans
2 tablespoons brown sugar

Rinse the grapes and pat dry. Combine the cream cheese, sour cream, granulated sugar and vanilla in a large bowl and mix well. Add the grapes and mix well. Stir in the pecans and brown sugar. Spoon into a serving bowl. Chill, covered, until serving time.

"EASY LIKE SUNDAY MORNING" SALAD

SERVES *6* TO *8*

TANGY VINAIGRETTE
1 cup vegetable oil
1/2 to 1 cup sugar
1/2 cup apple cider vinegar
1 tablespoon soy sauce
1 teaspoon salt

SALAD
2 bunches red leaf lettuce
2 (3-ounce) packages ramen noodles, crumbled and toasted
1 cup slivered almonds, toasted

To prepare the vinaigrette, combine the oil, sugar, vinegar, soy sauce and salt in a jar with a tight-fitting lid and shake to mix well.

To prepare the salad, rinse the lettuce and pat dry. Tear the lettuce into bite-size pieces and place in a salad bowl. Discard the seasoning packets from the ramen noodles or reserve for another use. Add the ramen noodles and almonds to the lettuce. Pour one-half of the vinaigrette over the salad and toss to coat. Serve immediately. Store the remaining vinaigrette in the refrigerator.

BROAD STREET BROCCOLI SALAD

SERVES 8

3 cups broccoli florets
1/2 cup (2 ounces) shredded Cheddar cheese
1/3 cup raisins
1/4 cup chopped red onion
1/2 cup light mayonnaise
2 tablespoons sugar
2 teaspoons lemon juice
8 slices bacon, crisp-cooked and crumbled

Combine the broccoli, cheese, raisins and onion in a large bowl and mix well. Whisk the mayonnaise, sugar and lemon juice in a small bowl until smooth. Add to the salad just before serving and toss to mix well. Stir in the bacon. Serve immediately.

GREEK ISLES POTATO SALAD

SERVES 10

2 pounds red potatoes or new potatoes,
cut into quarters
1 cup crumbled feta cheese
1/2 cup chopped green onions
1 tablespoon coarsely ground pepper
1/4 cup fresh lemon juice
1/4 cup extra-virgin olive oil

Cook the potatoes in water to cover in a saucepan until tender. Drain the potatoes and place in a large mixing bowl. Add the cheese, green onions, pepper, lemon juice and olive oil to the warm potatoes and mix well. Adjust the lemon juice, olive oil and pepper to taste. Serve warm, at room temperature or cold.

ELEGANTLY FRESH EGG SALAD
SERVES 4

8 slices bacon, cut into 1/4-inch pieces
4 shallots, minced
12 hard-cooked eggs, cut into 1/2-inch pieces
2/3 cup mayonnaise
1/2 cup coarsely chopped watercress leaves
1/2 cup minced chives
2 tablespoons minced fresh parsley leaves
4 teaspoons Dijon mustard
4 teaspoons lemon juice or white wine vinegar
2 pinches of salt
2 pinches of pepper
8 to 12 thin slices pumpernickel bread or bread of choice

Cook the bacon in a skillet over medium heat for 5 minutes or until brown and crisp. Remove the bacon to paper towels to drain. Drain the skillet, reserving 1 tablespoon of the bacon drippings. Add the shallots to the reserved drippings in the skillet. Cook for 5 minutes or until soft and brown. Combine the bacon, shallots, eggs, mayonnaise, watercress, chives, parsley, Dijon mustard, lemon juice, salt and pepper in a medium bowl and mix well. Serve on the bread as sandwiches.

NOTE: The salad may be chilled, covered, for 8 to 10 hours before serving.

Many organizations all over Chattanooga have benefited from the League's influence through the years. One such agency is Allied Arts; the League was instrumental in organizing the first Allied Arts Council in 1958 and promoted the first Allied Arts Festival in 1960. Today, Allied Arts of Greater Chattanooga is a private, nonprofit arts fund and council that provides a united voice for all cultural organizations and activities in Hamilton County.

PORCH PARTY PASTA SALAD

SERVES 8

DIJON TARRAGON VINAIGRETTE
3/4 cup olive oil
1/2 cup tarragon vinegar
1 teaspoon Dijon mustard
3/4 teaspoon salt, or to taste
1/2 teaspoon pepper
1/2 teaspoon garlic powder, or 1 small garlic clove, minced
1/4 teaspoon sugar

SALAD
2 cups chopped cooked chicken breasts (optional)
1 pound rotini, cooked and drained
8 ounces bacon, crisp-cooked and chopped
1 bunch fresh spinach, cut into chiffonade
1/2 cup black olives
1 cup (4 ounces) shredded Monterey Jack cheese
1/2 cup crumbled bleu cheese

To prepare the vinaigrette, whisk the olive oil, vinegar, Dijon mustard, salt, pepper, garlic powder and sugar in a small bowl until smooth.

To prepare the salad, combine the chicken, pasta, bacon, spinach, olives, Monterey Jack cheese and bleu cheese in a large bowl and mix well. Drizzle one-half of the vinaigrette over the pasta mixture and toss to coat. Add the remaining vinaigrette to taste.

Photograph for this recipe appears on page 29.

"Spring Chicken" Salad

Serves 4

1 pound boneless skinless chicken breasts
1 cup dry white wine
1/2 teaspoon salt
1 teaspoon pepper

1/2 cup mayonnaise (for this recipe,
   Duke's brand was used for testing)
1/2 cup green grapes
1/2 cup coarsely chopped walnuts
Salt and pepper to taste

Place the chicken, wine, 1/2 teaspoon salt and 1 teaspoon pepper in a sealable plastic bag. Seal the bag and turn to coat. Marinate in the refrigerator for 3 to 10 hours. Place the chicken in a baking dish. Bake in a preheated 350-degree oven for 35 to 40 minutes or until the chicken is cooked through. Remove from the oven to cool. Cut the chicken into large pieces. Pulse the chicken and mayonnaise in a food processor just until it begins to mix. Add the grapes and walnuts. Pulse until combined and of the desired consistency. Sprinkle with salt and pepper to taste.

NOTE: Obviously, dark meat can be substituted in this recipe.

> ### THE DARK MEAT YEARS
>
> *In the 1990s the League was approached by* Good Morning America *inquiring into a rumor that someone was banned from admission after rebelliously serving chicken salad with dark meat. League president Christine Smith politely denied the rumor's accuracy. After hearing this story, one shocked member offered to serve the* GMA *crew her mother's positively delicious dark meat chicken salad, intending to refute the tale and restore the League's good name. Although tempted, the League ultimately decided it was best to let sleeping chickens lie!*

Oriental Flank Steak

Serves 4 to 6

1 1/2 pounds flank steak
5 green onions, chopped
3/4 cup vegetable oil
1/2 cup soy sauce

1 1/2 teaspoons ginger
1 1/2 teaspoons garlic powder
3 tablespoons honey
2 tablespoons vinegar

Place the steak in a large shallow dish or sealable plastic bag. Combine the green onions, oil, soy sauce, ginger, garlic powder, honey and vinegar in a bowl and mix well. Pour over the steak. Cover the dish or seal the bag. Marinate in the refrigerator for 8 to 10 hours, turning the steak once.

Drain the steak, reserving the marinade. Place the steak on a grill rack. Grill over preheated hot coals for 5 to 10 minutes on each side or to the desired degree of doneness, basting frequently with the reserved marinade. Cut the steak across the grain into thick slices to serve.

PARTY PORK TENDERLOIN

SERVES 8 TO 10

1 cup soy sauce
1/2 cup sherry
1/2 cup firmly packed brown sugar
1/8 teaspoon pepper
1 purple onion, chopped
2 (1-pound) boneless pork tenderloins

Combine the soy sauce, sherry, brown sugar, pepper and onion in a bowl and mix well. Place the pork in a shallow dish. Pour the marinade over the pork. Marinate, covered, in the refrigerator for 2 to 10 hours. Bake in a preheated 400-degree oven for 30 minutes or until the pork tests done. Cut into 1×2 1/2-inch slices. Serve warm or at room temperature.

NOTE: The pork may be grilled for 15 minutes on each side or until the pork tests done.

PORK TENDERLOIN WITH TEXAS PESTO

SERVES 5

1 (1 1/2-pound) pork tenderloin
3 garlic cloves, minced
1/2 yellow onion, cut into chunks
1/2 cup loosely packed chopped fresh cilantro
2 tablespoons fresh lime juice
1 teaspoon canned chopped jalapeño chiles
2 tablespoons corn oil or vegetable oil
1/2 cup (2 ounces) finely shredded Monterey Jack cheese

Cut the tenderloin lengthwise to, but not through, the other side. Open like a book and lay flat between two sheets of waxed paper. Pound 1/2 to 1/4 inch thick with a meat mallet. Pulse the garlic, onion, cilantro, lime juice and jalapeño chiles in a food processor until coarsely chopped. Add the corn oil gradually, processing constantly for 10 to 15 seconds or until mostly smooth. Spread one-half of the pesto over the tenderloin and top with the cheese. Roll up the tenderloin tightly lengthwise to form a log, using the waxed paper to help. Secure with kitchen twine. Spread the remaining pesto over the top of the tenderloin.

Place the tenderloin on a rack in a roasting pan. Bake in a preheated 400-degree oven for 55 to 60 minutes or to 160 degrees on a meat thermometer. Cool for 5 minutes. Discard the string. Cut the tenderloin into slices and serve. Serve with Heirloom Salsa Verde (page 19) on the side.

"Lazy Susan's" Rack Of Lamb

Serves 4 to 6

1/2 teaspoon garlic
1 teaspoon salt
1/2 teaspoon pepper
1/2 teaspoon ginger
1 bay leaf, crumbled
1/2 teaspoon thyme
1/2 teaspoon sage
1/2 teaspoon marjoram
1 1/2 tablespoons soy sauce
1 tablespoon vegetable oil
2 small racks of lamb

Combine the garlic, salt, pepper, ginger, bay leaf, thyme, sage, marjoram, soy sauce and oil in a bowl and mix well. Rub the lamb with the herb mixture and place in a shallow dish. Marinate, covered, in the refrigerator for 2 hours. Place the lamb bone side down on a rack in a roasting pan. Roast in a preheated 450-degree oven for 30 to 40 minutes or until the lamb tests done.

NOTE: The lamb may also be grilled.

Yummy Rib Method!

Clean the ribs and remove the membrane from the underside, being careful to only remove the thin top membrane and not the fat it is attached to. Pat the ribs dry. Coat generously with your favorite rub and massage into the pork well. Wrap in plastic wrap. Chill for 8 to 10 hours.

Discard the plastic wrap. Place each rack of ribs on top of two ice cubes on a large sheet of heavy-duty foil and wrap tightly to seal. Place the foil packet on a baking sheet or in a shallow roasting pan. Bake in a preheated 250-degree oven for 2 3/4 to 3 hours. Unwrap the ribs and rub with your favorite barbecue sauce. Place on a grill rack. Grill over low heat for 15 to 20 minutes per side.

COLD LEMON CHICKEN

SERVES 6 TO 12

1/4 cup (1/2 stick) butter
12 boneless skinless chicken breasts
1/2 cup (or more) dry vermouth
1/2 cup fresh lemon juice
1/2 teaspoon salt
1/4 teaspoon white pepper
1/4 cup fresh lemon juice
1 1/2 cups mayonnaise
1/4 cup chopped parsley for garnish
12 lemon slices for garnish
12 black olive slices for garnish
1 1/2 to 2 cups watercress

Melt the butter in a skillet. Add the chicken and sauté until golden brown. Remove the chicken and place in a heavy flame-proof baking dish with a lid. Add the vermouth to the pan drippings in the skillet. Cook over high heat until the liquid is reduced to 1/3 cup. Remove from the heat. Add 1/2 cup lemon juice, the salt and white pepper. Pour over the chicken. Bake, covered, in a preheated 350-degree oven for 30 minutes or until tender and cooked through, basting with the pan drippings and adding additional vermouth if needed. Remove the chicken to a serving platter.

Cook the pan drippings over high heat until the liquid is reduced by one-half. Pour over the chicken and cool to room temperature. Cover tightly and chill for 8 to 10 hours.

Whisk 1/4 cup lemon juice and the mayonnaise in a bowl until smooth. Dip the chicken in the mayonnaise mixture and return to the serving platter. Pour the remaining mayonnaise mixture carefully over the chicken. Garnish the top of each chicken breast with the parsley, a lemon slice and olive slice. Chill several hours before serving. Just before serving, arrange the watercress around the edge of the platter.

PAN-SEARED TARRAGON CHICKEN

SERVES 4

1¹/2 tablespoons butter
1¹/2 tablespoons olive oil
4 boneless skinless chicken breasts
Salt and pepper to taste
1 shallot, minced
¹/2 cup vermouth

¹/2 cup heavy cream
¹/4 cup low-sodium chicken broth
1 tablespoon fresh tarragon
1 tablespoon fresh lemon juice
1 tablespoon fresh tarragon for garnish

Melt the butter with the olive oil in a large skillet over high heat. Season the chicken with salt and pepper and add to the skillet. Cook for 5 minutes on each side or until a nice crust develops. Cover the skillet and reduce the heat to medium. Cook for 5 minutes longer or until the chicken is cooked through. Remove the chicken with a slotted spoon to a serving platter or to individual plates and keep warm.

Cook the shallot in the pan drippings over medium-high heat for 15 seconds. Add the vermouth, stirring with a wooden spoon to scrape up all the brown bits. Cook for 3 to 5 minutes or until the liquid is reduced and thickened, stirring constantly. Add the cream, broth and 1 tablespoon tarragon. Cook for 3 to 5 minutes or until the liquid is reduced and thickened, stirring constantly. Adjust the seasonings to taste. Remove from the heat. Stir in the lemon juice and pour over the cooked chicken. Garnish with 1 tablespoon tarragon.

Photograph for this recipe appears on page 15.

SUPPER CLUB CASSEROLE

SERVES 8

1 chicken, cooked
1 cup (2 sticks) butter or margarine
¹/2 cup all-purpose flour
3¹/2 cups milk
¹/2 teaspoon salt
¹/4 teaspoon cayenne pepper
1 garlic clove, minced
2 ounces sharp Cheddar cheese, shredded

3 ounces Gruyère cheese, grated
1 (8-ounce) can button mushrooms, drained
2 (8-ounce) cans artichoke hearts, drained and cut into halves
1 cup crisp rice cereal
2 tablespoons butter, melted

Cut the chicken into bite-size pieces, discarding the skin and bones. Melt 1 cup butter in a saucepan over medium-low heat. Stir in the flour gradually. Cook until thickened, stirring constantly. Stir in the milk gradually. Cook until smooth and thickened, stirring constantly. Add the salt, cayenne pepper, garlic, Cheddar cheese and Gruyère cheese. Cook over low heat until the cheese melts and the sauce is bubbly. Stir in the mushrooms.

Layer the chicken and artichoke hearts in a buttered 9×13-inch baking dish. Pour the sauce over the layers. Toss the cereal with 2 tablespoons melted butter and sprinkle over the top. Bake in a preheated 350-degree oven for 30 minutes or until bubbly.

GREEK TURKEY BURGERS

SERVES 8

2 pounds lean ground turkey
2 (10-ounce) packages frozen chopped spinach,
thawed and squeezed dry
1/2 small onion, finely chopped
8 ounces feta cheese, chopped
1 garlic clove, finely chopped
2 teaspoons horseradish
2 tablespoons soy sauce
1 teaspoon pepper

Combine the turkey, spinach, onion, cheese, garlic, horseradish, soy sauce and pepper in a large bowl and mix well. Shape into eight 6-ounce patties. Place on a grill rack. Grill on a preheated grill on both sides until the liquid runs clear when pierced with a fork. Serve on sandwich buns with the desired condiments.

BATTERED SHRIMP

SERVES 8

1 cup all-purpose flour
1 tablespoon salt
1 teaspoon black pepper
1 teaspoon crushed red pepper
2 eggs
1 cup milk
1 pound shrimp, peeled and deveined
All-purpose flour
Vegetable oil for deep-frying

Combine 1 cup flour, the salt, black pepper, red pepper, eggs and milk in a large bowl and beat until smooth. Stir in the shrimp. Soak in the batter in the refrigerator for 1 hour or longer. Drain the shrimp, discarding the batter. Roll the shrimp in additional flour to coat. Deep-fry in hot oil in a large saucepan until golden brown.

NOTE: This batter is excellent for **Battered Steak Strips** as well. Cut a tenderized 1-pound round steak into 3×4- or 5-inch strips. Add to the batter and soak in the refrigerator for 1 hour or longer. Drain the steak, roll in the additional flour and deep-fry.

ROASTED FENNEL AND RED ONION SALMON

SERVES 4 TO 6

1/2 teaspoon fennel seeds
1 large red onion, cut into 1/2-inch wedges
6 garlic cloves
1 cup cherry tomatoes
1/2 teaspoon kosher salt

1/4 teaspoon pepper
2 teaspoons extra-virgin olive oil
4 to 6 salmon fillets, skin removed
1 large lemon, cut into halves
1/2 teaspoon kosher salt
1/4 teaspoon pepper

Toss the fennel seeds, onion, garlic, tomatoes, 1/2 teaspoon kosher salt, 1/4 teaspoon pepper and the olive oil together in a large bowl. Spread evenly in a roasting pan. Roast in a preheated 400-degree oven for 20 minutes. Move the vegetables to the side of the pan and add the salmon. Redistribute the vegetables around the salmon. Squeeze the lemon halves over the salmon. Sprinkle with 1/2 teaspoon kosher salt and 1/4 teaspoon pepper. Roast for 10 to 12 minutes or until the salmon flakes easily and is the same color throughout. Serve immediately.

EGGPLANT AND TOMATO GRATIN

SERVES 4

2 large ripe tomatoes, cut into 1/2-inch-thick slices
1/2 teaspoon salt
2 large eggplant, cut into 1/2-inch-thick slices
1/4 cup unseasoned dry bread crumbs
3/4 teaspoon dried oregano
3/4 teaspoon dried basil

2 garlic cloves, finely chopped
Salt to taste
1/2 cup fat-free half-and-half
1 1/2 cups (6 ounces) reduced-fat shredded mozzarella cheese
1/2 cup (2 ounces) freshly grated Parmesan cheese

Place the tomatoes in a single layer over paper towels. Sprinkle with 1/2 teaspoon salt and let stand for 30 minutes. Pat dry with paper towels, removing as much of the liquid as possible. Coat both sides of the eggplant slices with nonstick cooking spray. Place on a baking sheet. Broil under a preheated broiler for 5 minutes on each side or until tender. Sprinkle the bread crumbs in a baking dish coated with nonstick cooking spray. Arrange the eggplant in a single layer over the bread crumbs. Top with a single layer of tomatoes. Sprinkle with the oregano, basil, garlic and salt to taste. Drizzle with the half-and-half. Sprinkle with the mozzarella cheese and Parmesan cheese. Bake, covered with foil, in a preheated 350-degree oven for 45 minutes. Remove the foil and bake for 10 minutes longer.

SECOND HONEYMOON CURRY

SERVES 2 TO 4

1 cup finely chopped onion
1 cup finely chopped green apple
1 cup chopped eggplant
1/4 cup canola oil
1 garlic clove, crushed, or to taste
2 1/2 tablespoons curry powder
1 (1/2-inch) piece fresh ginger, chopped
1/4 cup ketchup
2 cups chicken stock
2 tablespoons fresh lemon juice
Salt to taste
Hot cooked long grain fine basmati rice

Cook the onion, apple and eggplant in the canola oil in a saucepan until soft. Add the garlic, curry powder, ginger, ketchup, stock and lemon juice and mix well. Season with salt. Cook until heated through. Serve over basmati rice.

ARTICHOKE PENNE

SERVES 6 TO 8

3 tablespoons butter
1/4 cup minced onion
1 garlic clove, minced
8 ounces sliced fresh mushrooms
1 cup artichoke hearts, chopped
1 cup heavy whipping cream
2 tablespoons capers, drained
Kosher salt and freshly ground pepper to taste
12 ounces penne, cooked and drained
3/4 cup (3 ounces) freshly grated Parmesan cheese
2 tablespoons chopped fresh parsley
4 slices bacon, crisp-cooked and crumbled (optional)

Melt the butter in a skillet over medium-high heat. Add the onion and garlic and sauté until tender. Add the mushrooms and sauté for 5 minutes. Stir in the artichokes. Cook for 2 to 3 minutes or until heated through. Spoon into a bowl and set aside.

Return the skillet to the heat and add the cream. Boil until the cream is reduced by half. Add the capers and artichoke mixture and mix well. Season with kosher salt and pepper. Pour over the warm pasta in a bowl and toss to coat. Stir in the cheese and parsley. Sprinkle with the bacon and serve immediately.

GREEN BEAN BUNDLES

SERVES 10 TO 15

2 pounds fresh green beans, trimmed
1 pound bacon, cut into halves
1 cup packed light brown sugar
2 tablespoons light soy sauce
1/2 teaspoon garlic powder
1/2 cup (1 stick) butter

Cook the green beans in boiling water in a large saucepan for 5 minutes. Drain and plunge immediately into cold water to stop the cooking process. Wrap eight to ten green beans with one piece of bacon, twisting the ends of the bacon and securing with a wooden pick. Place in a dish. Repeat with the remaining green beans and bacon.

Combine the brown sugar, soy sauce, garlic powder and butter in a microwave-safe dish and mix well. Microwave on High until blended, stirring twice. Pour over the green bean bundles. Marinate in the refrigerator for 24 hours.

Place the green bean bundles in a single layer in a baking dish. Reheat any marinade that has hardened in the dish and pour over the bundles. Bake in a preheated 350-degree oven for 30 minutes. Broil under a preheated broiler for 5 minutes.

GARLIC GINGER CARROTS

SERVES 4

2 garlic cloves, minced
1 pound carrots, peeled and sliced
1 tablespoon butter
1 teaspoon minced fresh ginger
1 tablespoon chopped cilantro
1/2 teaspoon grated lime zest
1 tablespoon fresh lime juice
1/4 teaspoon salt

Let the garlic stand for 10 minutes before using. Steam the carrots, covered, in a steamer over boiling water in a saucepan for 10 minutes or until tender. Melt the butter in a large nonstick skillet over medium heat. Add the garlic and ginger. Cook for 1 minute, stirring constantly. Remove from the heat. Stir in the carrots, cilantro, lime zest, lime juice and salt.

To freshen up carrots that seem to have lost their "snap," either store them in water in a dish in the refrigerator, or soak them in cold water for an hour to restore them.

DECADENT CAULIFLOWER GRATIN

SERVES 4 TO 6

1 large head cauliflower, cored and chopped (about 2^1/$_2$ pounds)
2 garlic cloves, minced
1 cup (or more) chicken stock
1^1/$_2$ teaspoons salt
^{1}/$_4$ cup (or more) heavy cream
2 tablespoons butter
^{1}/$_2$ cup (2 ounces) grated Parmigiano-Reggiano cheese
Salt to taste
^{1}/$_4$ cup (1 ounce) grated Gruyère cheese

Bring the cauliflower, garlic, stock and 1^1/$_2$ teaspoons salt just to a boil in a large saucepan over medium-high heat. Cover and reduce the heat. Simmer for 10 to 15 minutes or until the cauliflower is soft. Remove from the heat. Add the cream and butter. Purée with an emulsion blender or in a food processor or blender. Stir in the Parmigiano-Reggiano cheese. Season with salt to taste. Spoon into a baking dish. Top with the Gruyère cheese. Broil under a preheated broiler until brown, watching carefully to prevent overbrowning.

VOLUNTEER VIDALIA SOUFFLÉ

SERVES 6 TO 8

3 large Vidalia onions, chopped
^{1}/$_4$ cup (^{1}/$_2$ stick) butter
3 eggs
1 cup sour cream
1 tablespoon cayenne pepper
^{1}/$_2$ cup (2 ounces) freshly grated Parmesan cheese

Sauté the onions in the butter in a skillet until soft. Spoon into a deep-dish pie plate. Combine the eggs, sour cream, cayenne pepper and cheese in a bowl and mix well. Pour over the onions. Bake in a preheated 450-degree oven for 15 minutes. Reduce the oven temperature to 325 degrees. Bake for 20 minutes longer. Let stand for 15 minutes before serving.

SPRING PEAS

SERVES 4

2 tablespoons olive oil
1 shallot, minced
1 garlic clove, minced or pressed
1 (16-ounce) package frozen baby peas
1/4 cup heavy cream
1/4 teaspoon sugar
2 tablespoons minced fresh tarragon
1 tablespoon unsalted butter
2 teaspoons white wine vinegar or Champagne vinegar
Salt and pepper to taste

Heat the olive oil in a large skillet over medium-high heat. Add the shallot. Cook for 2 minutes or until soft. Add the garlic. Cook for 2 minutes or until fragrant. Stir in the peas, cream and sugar. Cook, covered, for 5 minutes or until the peas are heated through and still bright green. Stir in the tarragon and butter. Remove from the heat. Stir in the vinegar. Adjust the seasonings to taste. Season with salt and pepper and serve.

Photograph for this recipe appears on page 15.

39

BEEF'S BEST FRIEND

SERVES 6 TO 8

8 potatoes, baked
1/4 cup (1/2 stick) butter, softened
1 (10-ounce) can cream of chicken soup
1 cup sour cream
1 small onion, chopped
11/2 cups (6 ounces) shredded mild Cheddar cheese
Salt and pepper to taste
Paprika to taste

Cut each potato into halves. Scoop out the potato pulp and place in a bowl. Mash the potatoes. Add the butter, soup, sour cream, onion and cheese and mix well. Add salt and pepper. Stir in paprika. Spoon into a lightly greased 21/2-quart baking dish. Bake in a preheated 350-degree oven for 30 to 40 minutes or until light brown on top.

NOTE: As an alternative, you may boil the potatoes. Peel the hot potatoes and place in a bowl. Proceed as directed.

FRIED GREEN TOMATOES

SERVES 8 TO 10

4 or 5 green tomatoes	2 cups crushed crackers
1 egg	(about 1 1/2 sleeves)
2 tablespoons water	2 teaspoons salt
2 cups buttermilk	Freshly ground pepper to taste
2 teaspoons salt	4 cups vegetable oil
2 cups all-purpose flour	

Cut the tomatoes into 1/4-inch-thick slices. Mix the egg, water, buttermilk and 2 teaspoons salt in a medium bowl. Add the tomatoes. Soak in the refrigerator for 1 hour or cover and soak for 4 to 5 hours.

Mix the flour, crackers, 2 teaspoons salt and pepper in a bowl. Heat the oil in a deep skillet over high heat. Coat the tomato slices one at a time with the flour mixture, pressing so the coating will adhere. Fry one layer of tomato slices at a time in the hot oil until golden brown, turning with a fork. Lift each tomato slice with a fork and let the excess oil drip back into the skillet. Place on paper towels to drain.

NOTE: **Fried Okra** may be prepared the same way. Chop the okra into 1/4- to 1/2-inch pieces and add to the batter. Scoop the okra out of the batter with a big slotted spoon, letting some of the batter drain off. Drop into the flour mixture and turn to coat well. Add the okra pieces one at a time by hand to the hot oil and fry until golden brown. Drain on paper towels.

FRESH TOMATO TART

SERVES 8 TO 10

3 or 4 ripe tomatoes	Pepper to taste
Salt to taste	1 tablespoon extra-virgin olive oil
1 refrigerator pie pastry	1 cup (4 ounces) shredded
2 cups (8 ounces) shredded	mozzarella cheese
mozzarella cheese	Chopped fresh basil for garnish
2 tablespoons chopped fresh basil	

Slice the tomatoes. Sprinkle with salt and place on paper towels to drain well. Line a 10-inch tart pan with a removable bottom with the pie pastry, trimming the edges. Bake in a preheated 400-degree oven for 5 minutes. Remove from the oven. Maintain the oven temperature. Spread 2 cups cheese over the bottom of the hot crust. Season with 2 tablespoons basil. Arrange the tomato slices as evenly as possible over the top to cover. Season with salt and pepper. Drizzle with the olive oil. Sprinkle with 1 cup cheese. Bake for 20 to 25 minutes or until heated through. Garnish with chopped fresh basil. Cut into wedges and serve warm or at room temperature.

GOUDA GRITS

SERVES 4 TO 6

2 cups chicken broth
2 1/2 cups water
1 cup quick-cooking grits
1 1/2 cups (6 ounces) shredded smoked Gouda cheese
1 tablespoon butter
1 cup steamed asparagus tips (about 1 bunch)
Salt and pepper to taste

Bring the broth and water to a boil in a saucepan. Add the grits. Cook until creamy, stirring frequently. Stir in the cheese. Cook unil the cheese is melted, stirring occasionally. Add the butter and asparagus. Season with salt and pepper.

NOTE: To make this dish a meal, spoon the grits into serving bowls and make a round indentation in the center. Fill with either black-eyed peas or small shrimp that have been boiled in beer.

"HAND ME DOWN" SPOON BREAD

SERVES 4 TO 6

3/4 cup yellow cornmeal
1/4 cup all-purpose flour
1 tablespoon butter
3/4 teaspoon salt
1 tablespoon sugar
1 teaspoon baking powder
1 egg
2 cups milk
2 tablespoons butter

Mix the cornmeal, flour, 1 tablespoon butter, the salt, sugar and baking powder in a bowl. Beat in the egg and 1 cup of the milk. Melt 2 tablespoons butter in an 8×8-inch baking dish in a preheated 375-degree oven. Add the batter. Pour the remaining 1 cup milk over the top. Bake for 45 minutes or until the top is crusty. Serve hot.

RIVER QUEEN CARROT CAKE

SERVES 20 TO 25

CAKE
2 cups all-purpose flour
2 teaspoons baking soda
2 teaspoons cinnamon
1 teaspoon salt
2 cups sugar
2 cups fresh baby carrots
1¼ cups vegetable oil
4 eggs

CREAM CHEESE FROSTING
8 ounces cream cheese, softened
½ cup (1 stick) butter, softened
1 (1-pound) package confectioners' sugar
8 ounces chopped pecans

To prepare the cake, grease and lightly flour two 9-inch cake pans. Line the prepared pans with waxed paper. Stir the flour, baking soda, cinnamon, salt and sugar together in a large bowl. Process the carrots in a food processor until finely ground. Mix the carrots, oil and eggs in a bowl. Add to the flour mixture and beat well. Spoon the batter into the prepared pans. Bake in a preheated 350-degree oven for 45 minutes. Cool in the pans for 10 minutes. Invert onto wire racks to cool completely. Remove the waxed paper.

To prepare the frosting, beat the cream cheese and butter in a mixing bowl until smooth. Add the confectioners' sugar gradually, beating constantly. Stir in the pecans. Spread between the layers and over the top of the cake.

NOTE: To garnish, create a nest with flaked coconut, sprinkle with green candy sugar, and fill with pastel candy eggs.

Photograph for this recipe appears at right.

CRUMB COATING A CAKE

For a flawlessly frosted cake, set aside some of the icing to be used to frost the cake and thin it with several drops of water. Spread the thinned icing all over the cake and allow it to dry for 10 minutes. Then frost the cake as normal with the rest of the icing. Crumb Coating a cake provides a seal, keeping loose bits of cake from mixing in with the icing…especially handy for dark cakes with light-colored frosting.

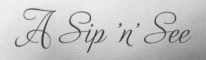

A Sip 'n' See

Lemon Drop Punch

Artichoke Melbas

Topplin' Tomatoes

Bleu Cheese Bacon Puffs

Porch Party Pasta Salad

Crab Quiche

River Queen Carrot Cake

Frosted Banana Cookies

Jam Cake

Serves 8 to 10

Cake

4 cups all-purpose flour
1 tablespoon baking soda
1 teaspoon ground cloves
1 teaspoon cinnamon
1 teaspoon ground allspice
2 cups sugar
1 cup (2 sticks) butter, softened
6 medium eggs
1 cup buttermilk
1 cup chopped pecans
1 apple, peeled and grated
2 cups blackberry jam (with or without seeds)

Caramel Glaze

3 cups packed light brown sugar
3/4 cup (1 1/2 sticks) butter
3/4 cup evaporated milk
1/2 to 1 cup (or more) confectioners' sugar

To prepare the cake, sift the flour, baking soda, cloves, cinnamon and allspice together twice. Cream the sugar and butter in a mixing bowl until smooth. Add the eggs and beat well. Add the flour mixture and buttermilk alternately, mixing well after each addition. Add the pecans and apple and mix well. Fold in the jam. Spoon into three well greased and floured 9-inch cake pans. Bake in a preheated 350-degree oven for 40 to 45 minutes or until the layers test done. Cool in the pans for 10 minutes. Invert onto wire racks to cool completely.

To prepare the glaze, mix the brown sugar, butter and evaporated milk in a 3-quart saucepan. Bring to a rolling boil. Boil for 3 minutes. Remove from the heat to cool slightly. Beat in the confectioners' sugar until smooth and of a glaze consistency. Pour between the layers and over the top of the cake, letting the glaze drizzle down the side.

Six-Flavor Pound Cake

Serves 12 or more

Cake

3 cups sifted all-purpose flour
1/2 teaspoon baking powder
3 cups sugar
1 cup (2 sticks) butter, softened
1/2 cup shortening
5 eggs
1 teaspoon vanilla extract
1 teaspoon coconut extract
1 teaspoon almond extract
1 teaspoon lemon extract
1 teaspoon rum extract
1 teaspoon vanilla butter nut extract
1 cup evaporated milk

Six-Flavor Glaze

1 cup sugar
1/2 cup water
1/2 teaspoon vanilla extract
1/2 teaspoon coconut extract
1/2 teaspoon almond extract
1/2 teaspoon lemon extract
1/2 teaspoon rum extract
1/2 teaspoon vanilla butter nut extract

To prepare the cake, mix the flour and baking powder together. Cream the sugar, butter and shortening at medium speed in a mixing bowl until light and fluffy. Add the eggs one at a time, beating well after each addition. Add the flavorings one at a time, mixing well after each addition. Add the flour mixture and evaporated milk alternately, beating constantly at low speed. Pour into a greased and floured 10-inch tube pan. Bake in a preheated 300-degree oven for 1 1/2 hours.

To prepare the glaze, combine the sugar, water and flavorings in a saucepan and mix well. Cook over low heat until the sugar dissolves, stirring constantly. Let stand until cool.

To assemble, pierce the top of the warm cake with a wooden pick. Pour the cooled glaze over the top of the cake in the pan. Let stand for 15 to 20 minutes. Invert onto a cake plate and cool completely.

SPICED PINEAPPLE CRISP

SERVES 6

1 (16-ounce) can pineapple chunks
2/3 cup sugar
1/3 cup vinegar
1 teaspoon whole cloves
2 sticks cinnamon
1/4 cup all-purpose flour
1 cup (4 ounces) shredded sharp Cheddar cheese
1/4 cup (1/2 stick) butter, melted
1/3 (12-ounce) package butter crackers, crumbled

Drain the pineapple, reserving the juice in a saucepan. Add the sugar, vinegar, cloves and cinnamon to the juice and bring to a boil. Reduce the heat and simmer for 10 minutes. Pour over the pineapple in a bowl. Chill for several hours.

Drain the pineapple, reserving 1/4 cup of the liquid and discarding the cloves and cinnamon. Combine the flour with the reserved 1/4 cup liquid in a bowl and mix well. Stir in the cheese and pineapple. Spoon into a greased 8×8-inch baking dish. Mix the butter and cracker crumbs in a bowl. Sprinkle over the pineapple mixture. Bake in a preheated 350-degree oven for 30 minutes or until golden brown on top. Chill and serve.

> Representing almost five thousand acres of local and regional farms and more than two hundred rotating vendors each week, the Chattanooga Market is the region's largest producer-only market. Shoppers can find homegrown fruits, vegetables, flowers, and herbs, as well as gourmet chicken, beef, and lamb. Curb your hunger with farm-fresh cheeses, breads, jellies, salsas, candies, and more. Beginning in the spring and running through early winter, locals and tourists alike partake in this yummy Chattanooga tradition!

BLUEBERRY DELIGHT
SERVES 12

2 cups graham cracker crumbs
1/2 cup confectioners' sugar
1/2 cup (1 stick) butter or margarine, melted
1 cup chopped pecans
8 ounces cream cheese, softened
1 cup granulated sugar
2 eggs, beaten
2 teaspoons lemon juice
1 teaspoon vanilla extract
2 cups fresh or frozen blueberries
1 cup granulated sugar
1/4 cup water
3 tablespoons cornstarch
16 ounces whipped topping or whipped cream

Mix the graham cracker crumbs, confectioners' sugar, butter and pecans thoroughly in a bowl. Press over the bottom of a greased 9×13-inch baking pan. Beat the cream cheese, 1 cup granulated sugar, the eggs, lemon juice and vanilla in a mixing bowl until smooth. Pour over the graham cracker crust. Bake in a preheated 350-degree oven for 20 minutes. Cool completely.

Combine the blueberries, 1 cup granulated sugar, the water and cornstarch in a heavy saucepan and mix well. Cook over medium heat until thickened, stirring constantly. Remove from the heat to cool. Pour over the cooled layer. Top with whipped topping. Chill until serving time.

The Walnut Street Bridge is a perfect example of Chattanooga's dedication to preservation and revitalization. Built in 1891 and originally opened to motored vehicles, it is the oldest surviving truss bridge in the South. After 12 years of restoration, the Walnut Street Bridge is currently the longest pedestrian bridge in the world, spanning 2,730 feet. It is one of the city's most iconic features, providing breathtaking views of Coolidge Park, the Tennessee Aquarium, and the Riverfront.

CHOCOLATE TORTE

SERVES 10

5 ounces semisweet chocolate, chopped
3 ounces unsweetened chocolate, chopped
1/2 cup (1 stick) unsalted butter, cut into pieces
4 eggs, at room temperature
1/2 cup sugar
1/4 cup strong brewed scoffee, cooled to room temperature

1 tablespoon finely ground French roast coffee beans, sifted
1/4 teaspoon salt
1/4 cup all-purpose flour
1 cup heavy whipping cream
1 teaspoon vanilla extract
1/2 teaspoon sugar
Dash of cinnamon for garnish
Fresh blueberries for garnish

Butter an 8-inch cake pan and line with baking parchment. Butter the baking parchment and lightly flour. Melt the chocolates and butter in a small heavy saucepan over medium heat, stirring frequently. Whip the eggs, 1/2 cup sugar, the brewed coffee, ground coffee and salt at medium-high speed in the bowl of an electric mixer with the whip attachment for 8 minutes or until thick. Add the chocolate mixture. Beat at low speed until blended. Turn off the mixer. Sift the flour over the batter and fold in. Pour into the prepared pan. Bake in a preheated 350-degree oven for 25 to 30 minutes or until a cake tester inserted in the center comes out clean. Cool in the pan on a wire rack for 10 minutes. Place a plate over the torte and carefully invert onto the plate. Peel off the baking parchment. Flip the torte back onto the wire rack to cool completely.

Beat the whipping cream, vanilla and 1/2 teaspoon sugar in a mixing bowl until firm peaks form. Cut the cake into slices. Dollop each slice with the whipped cream. Garnish with cinnamon and blueberries.

CHOO CHOO CHOCOLATE PIE

SERVES 8

1 cup sugar
2 tablespoons baking cocoa
2 tablespoons cornstarch
1 cup milk
2 egg yolks

2 tablespoons butter
1 teaspoon vanilla extract
1 baked (9-inch) pie shell
2 cups heavy whipping cream
1/4 cup sugar

Mix 1 cup sugar, the baking cocoa and cornstarch in a saucepan. Add enough of the milk to just moisten the sugar mixture. Beat the egg yolks and remaining milk in a small bowl. Add to the sugar mixture and mix well. Cook over medium heat until thickened, stirring constantly. Add the butter and vanilla and mix well. Pour into the baked pie shell. Let stand until cool. Beat the whipping cream with 1/4 cup sugar in a mixing bowl until thick. Spoon over the top of the pie to cover. Store in the refrigerator.

BIG RIVER GRILLE AND BREWING WORKS
CHOCOLATE PEANUT BUTTER PIE

SERVES 10

2 cups chocolate sandwich cookie crumbs
(for this recipe, Oreos brand
was used for testing)
6 tablespoons butter, melted
16 ounces cream cheese, softened
1 cup peanut butter
1 teaspoon vanilla extract
1 cup confectioners' sugar

1 cup heavy whipping cream
16 ounces cream cheese, softened
1/2 cup heavy cream
4 ounces chocolate, finely chopped
1 teaspoon vanilla extract
1 cup confectioners' sugar
1 cup heavy whipping cream
1 1/2 cups chocolate fudge sauce, heated

Process the cookie crumbs in a food processor until the consistency of sand. Mix with the butter in a bowl. Press over the bottom of a springform pan. Bake in a preheated 350-degree oven for 12 minutes or until set.

Beat 16 ounces cream cheese in the bowl of a stand mixer fitted with the paddle attachment until soft. Add the peanut butter, 1 teaspoon vanilla and 1 cup confectioners' sugar and mix well, scraping the side of the bowl frequently. Whip 1 cup heavy whipping cream in a bowl to just past soft peaks. Fold into the peanut butter mixture.

Beat 16 ounces cream cheese in the bowl of a stand mixer fitted with the paddle attachment until soft. Bring 1/2 cup heavy cream to a boil in a saucepan. Pour over the chocolate in a bowl and stir until melted and smooth. Add the chocolate mixture, 1 teaspoon vanilla and 1 cup confectioners' sugar to the cream cheese and beat until smooth, scraping the side of the bowl frequently. Whip 1 cup heavy whipping cream in a bowl until just past soft peaks. Fold into the chocolate mixture.

Cut four-inch strips of baking parchment and line the inside edge of the springform pan. Spoon the peanut butter filling over the baked crust. Spread the chocolate filling on top of the peanut butter filling. Ladle the chocolate fudge sauce over the chocolate filling. Store in the freezer. Place in the refrigerator the day before serving.

Big River Grille and Brewing Works began in 1993 as a dream of bringing together fresh, handcrafted beer and made-from-scratch, world-class cuisine. Their passion is to produce a broad variety of items featuring bold flavors and fresh, innovative tastes that are cultivated through seasonal creations.

FROSTED BANANA COOKIES

MAKES 2 DOZEN

COOKIES

3/4 cup (1 1/2 sticks) margarine, softened
3/4 cup sugar
1 egg
1 teaspoon vanilla extract
2 ripe bananas, mashed
2 cups self-rising flour
1/2 teaspoon salt

BROWN SUGAR FROSTING

6 tablespoons brown sugar
1/4 cup (1/2 stick) margarine
1/4 cup milk
1/2 teaspoon vanilla extract
1 (1-pound) package confectioners' sugar
1 teaspoon yellow food coloring

To prepare the cookies, cream the margarine and sugar in a mixing bowl until light and fluffy. Add the egg, vanilla and bananas and mix well. Add a mixture of the flour and salt 1/2 cup at a time, beating well after each addition. Drop by teaspoonfuls onto an ungreased cookie sheet. Bake in a preheated 350-degree oven for 8 minutes. Remove to a wire rack to cool.

To prepare the frosting, bring the brown sugar, margarine, milk and vanilla to a boil in a saucepan. Remove from the heat. Beat in the confectioners' sugar until of the desired consistency. Add the food coloring and mix well. Add a few drops of water if the frosting becomes too thick. Frost the cooled cookies.

GERTRUDE OEHMIG'S
CARAMEL ICING

*MAKES ENOUGH ICING FOR
ONE (2-LAYER) CAKE OR
2 DOZEN CUPCAKES*

3 cups sugar
2 cups heavy cream
1/4 cup (1/2 stick) butter
1 tablespoon vanilla extract

Grease a heavy saucepan with butter. Combine the sugar, cream and butter in the prepared saucepan and mix well. Cook over low heat until the sugar dissolves, stirring constantly. Increase the heat to medium and bring to a full rolling boil, stirring constantly. Continue to cook until 234 to 240 degrees on a candy thermometer, soft-ball stage. This should take about 20 minutes. Remove from the heat and cool for 10 minutes. Beat in the vanilla. Continue to beat until the icing is of spreading consistency.

Miss Gertrude Oehmig introduced her famous icing at her Coffee Shop in the early 1900s and later served it at Loveman's Tea Room and Girls' Preparatory School. It is still a favorite in Chattanooga.

A Season of Hospitality

The summer heat brings an ambush of zucchini and tomatoes along with
a variety of indulgences for every craving, during which our not-so-little city
becomes a welcoming outdoor mecca. While the sun shines, fill the picnic basket
and spend the day in a lively park or on a secluded rock in the middle of a creek.
With the family in tow, head to one of the nearby farms for "U-pick" berries
or cool off with some fresh ice cream from a local dairy.

Summer is the most active time in the Scenic City, with enough pursuits to
satisfy any outdoor enthusiast. From triathlons and 100-mile bike races over
3 mountains in 3 states, to hang gliding and riding zip lines, to kayaking
and whitewater rafting, there's something for everyone to work up an appetite.

Parades, barbecues, and concerts make Chattanooga a special place to celebrate
the summer holidays. On the 4th of July, children's faces are full of delight
from sparklers while the booms of sky-high fireworks explode into magical lights
that glitter over the Tennessee River.

Though music fills the nights along the Riverfront and the sounds of
America's favorite pastime echo from the Lookouts' stadium, we think some of the
most memorable summer evenings are spent gathered in the backyard with friends
and family. It's a time for watermelon juice to drip through fingers,
for popsicle-covered kids to dash through sprinklers, and for using a mason jar
drained of sweet tea to catch lightening bugs. So get the crew together,
let dad fire up the grill, and celebrate the heat Southern style!

Summer

Picnic in the Park

Surefire Sangria
Sunshine Sauce
BLT Tartlets
Gazpacho
Below the Line Pimento Cheese
Signature "Fried" Chicken
Devil in Disguise Eggs
Creamy Lemonade Pie

MUSTARD SHRIMP

SERVES 8 TO 10

1/4 cup finely chopped parsley
1/4 cup finely chopped onion
1 cup finely chopped celery
1/4 cup tarragon vinegar
1/4 cup white wine vinegar
1/2 cup olive oil
3 tablespoons Dijon mustard

1 to 2 teaspoons crushed red pepper
flakes, or to taste
2 teaspoons salt
Black pepper to taste
1 1/2 pounds shrimp, cooked, peeled
and deveined

Combine the parsley, onion, celery, tarragon vinegar, white wine vinegar, olive oil, Dijon mustard, red pepper flakes, salt and black pepper in a medium bowl and mix well. Pour over the shrimp in a large bowl. Marinate, covered, in the refrigerator for 24 hours or longer, stirring occasionally. Drain the shrimp, discarding the marinade. Place the shrimp in a shallow serving dish. Serve with cocktail forks or wooden picks.

FIG IN A RIBBON

MAKES 28 BITES

14 small fresh figs, stemmed and
cut into halves
10 ounces gorgonzola cheese, crumbled
1 teaspoon finely chopped fresh rosemary

1/2 teaspoon pepper
4 ounces thinly sliced country ham, cut
into halves lengthwise
4 sprigs of fresh rosemary for garnish

Top each fig half evenly with some of the cheese. Sprinkle evenly with the chopped rosemary and pepper. Wrap the ham around each fig, securing with a wooden pick. Place seam side down on a foil-lined baking sheet. Bake in a preheated 350-degree oven for 10 minutes or until the cheese melts. Garnish with rosemary sprigs.

Photograph for this recipe appears on page 81.

During the 1800s, Chattanooga was host to lavish riverboats that drifted down the Tennessee River. In keeping with the area's history, excursions are available almost year-round on our Southern Belle. This five hundred-passenger riverboat has three viewing decks to choose from, permitting you to soak in local scenery and mountain views. If you are intrigued by the thought of lunch, high tea, or dinner on the river, this is a meal to remember!

BLT TARTLETS

SERVES 12

1 pound bacon, chopped
1 bunch green onions, chopped
3/4 cup mayonnaise
1 loaf thinly sliced white bread
1 package cherry tomatoes, sliced

Fry the bacon in a skillet until crisp; remove to paper towels to drain. Combine the bacon, green onions and mayonnaise in a small bowl and mix well. Chill in the refrigerator.

Cut each bread slice into three rounds using a 1- to 1 1/2-inch biscuit cutter. Place the bread rounds on a baking sheet. Bake in a preheated 300-degree oven for 15 to 20 minutes or until light brown and toasted. Let stand until cool. To serve, spoon the bacon mixture onto each bread round and top with a cherry tomato slice.

FIRECRACKERS

SERVES 12 TO 15

1 (16-ounce) package club crackers
1 1/4 cups canola oil
1 envelope ranch salad dressing mix
3 tablespoons crushed red pepper
Cayenne pepper to taste

Place the crackers in a large bowl. Whisk the canola oil, salad dressing mix, red pepper and cayenne pepper in a bowl. Pour over the crackers and toss carefully. Let stand until all of the mixture is absorbed, tossing occasionally.

NOTE: These are wonderful to take along to the lake for a spicy treat.

Rene's Boursin

SERVES 8 TO 10

8 ounces cream cheese, softened
1 garlic clove, crushed
1 teaspoon caraway seeds
1 teaspoon basil
1 teaspoon dill weed
1 teaspoon chives
1/4 to 1/2 cup lemon pepper

Combine the cream cheese, garlic, caraway seeds, basil, dill weed and chives and mix well. Shape into a ball or log. Roll in the lemon pepper. Serve with crackers.

Chutney Cheese

SERVES 15 TO 20

16 ounces cream cheese, softened
1/2 cup chutney
1/4 cup finely chopped green onions
1 garlic clove, minced
1 cup (4 ounces) shredded Colby-Jack cheese
Kosher salt and freshly ground pepper to taste
1 cup chopped pecans

Combine the cream cheese, chutney, green onions, garlic and Colby-Jack cheese in a bowl and mix well. Season with kosher salt and pepper. Shape into a ball and roll in the pecans to coat. Serve with crackers or bagel and pita crisps.

CHEESE SLAW

SERVES 15 TO 20

16 ounces Swiss cheese, coarsely shredded
1 bunch green onions with tops, chopped
$1/2$ cup chopped banana peppers
$1/2$ cup finely chopped jalapeño chiles
Mayonnaise to taste

Combine the cheese, green onions, banana peppers and jalapeño chiles in a bowl and mix well. Add enough mayonnaise to bind and mix well. Store in the refrigerator for up to 1 week. Add additional mayonnaise if needed. Serve in a hollowed-out cabbage with thin wheat crackers.

SUNSHINE SAUCE

SERVES 25

1 (18-ounce) jar apple jelly, at room temperature
1 (18-ounce) jar pineapple preserves, at room temperature
2 tablespoons plus 1 teaspoon horseradish, at room temperature
2 tablespoons Dijon mustard, at room temperature
2 teaspoons dry mustard
$3/4$ teaspoon kosher salt
8 ounces cream cheese

Combine the apple jelly, pineapple preserves, horseradish, Dijon mustard, dry mustard, and kosher salt in a medium bowl and mix with a whisk or fork until smooth. Place the cream cheese on a serving tray. Spoon the sauce over the cream cheese. Serve with water crackers.

A League member changed the name of this recipe from Jezebel Sauce and sweetened it a bit. She now serves it as a crowd-favorite at birthday parties, baby showers, and holidays.

TABLESIDE GUACAMOLE
SERVES 4 TO 6

ROASTED TOMATO AND JALAPEÑO CHILES
2 small jalapeño chiles
1 large tomato, chopped

GUACAMOLE
2 large ripe avocados
1 teaspoon sea salt
1/4 cup chopped fresh cilantro
2 tablespoons finely chopped red onion
Juice of 1/2 large lime
Juice of 1/4 large orange

To prepare the Roasted Tomato and Jalapeño Chiles, cut the jalapeño chiles into halves. Remove the seeds and membranes. Spread the tomato and jalapeño chiles on a baking sheet. Roast in a preheated 400-degree oven for 20 minutes or until the tomato is tender and the edges are brown and the jalapeño chiles are lightly charred. Remove from the oven to cool. Chop the jalapeño chiles. Mix with the tomato in an airtight container. Store, covered, in the refrigerator until serving time.

To prepare the guacamole, cut the avocados into halves and scoop into a bowl. Mash the avocados with the sea salt using two forks. Add 1/3 cup of the Roasted Tomato and Jalapeño Chiles, reserving any remainder for another purpose. Add the cilantro and onion and mix lightly. Stir in the lime juice and orange juice until of the desired consistency. Serve immediately with tortilla chips.

The roasted tomato mixture for this recipe can be made several days in advance, and different chiles (such as serrano, poblano, etc.) may be substituted depending on preference and availability.

For a quick tableside presentation, prepare all ingredients in advance and have ready to add to serving bowl as needed. This recipe doubles well for large groups.

CRANBERRY AVOCADO SALSA

SERVES 4

2 tablespoons honey
1 tablespoon fresh lime juice
1 jalapeño chile, minced
1/4 cup finely chopped red onion

2 ripe avocados, chopped
3/4 cup cranberries, cut into halves
2 tablespoons chopped fresh cilantro
Salt and pepper to taste

Whisk the honey, lime juice, jalapeño chile and onion together in a bowl. Add the avocados, cranberries, cilantro and onion mixture and mix well. Season with salt and pepper. Serve with tortilla chips.

PINEAPPLE UPSIDE-DOWN CAKE MARTINIS

SERVES 10 TO 14

1 (46-ounce) can pineapple juice, chilled
3 cups vanilla vodka, chilled

Grenadine
Maraschino cherries for garnish

Blend the pineapple juice and vodka in a pretty serving pitcher. Pour into martini glasses. Add a splash of grenadine to each and garnish with a maraschino cherry.

COSMOPOLITAN PUNCH

SERVES 12 TO 15

8 cups cranberry juice, chilled
1 cup orange juice, chilled
2 cups citron vodka, chilled
1/2 cup Triple Sec, chilled

1 lemon, sliced
1 lime, sliced
1 cup frozen cranberries
1 (2-liter) bottle ginger ale, chilled

Combine the cranberry juice, orange juice, vodka, Triple Sec, lemon, lime and cranberries in a punch bowl and mix well. Chill until serving time. Add the ginger ale just before serving. Ladle into punch cups.

SUREFIRE SANGRIA

SERVES 6 TO 8

1/2 cup brandy	1 large lemon, sliced
1/3 cup frozen lemonade concentrate	1 large orange, sliced
1/4 cup lemon juice	1 large lime, sliced
1/3 cup orange juice	8 large maraschino cherries
1 (750-milliliter) bottle dry red wine	Sugar to taste
1/2 cup Triple Sec	1 cup frozen pineapple chunks

Mix the brandy, lemonade concentrate, lemon juice, orange juice, wine and Triple Sec in a punch bowl or pitcher. Float the fruit slices and maraschino cherries in the mixture. Chill for 8 to 10 hours for optimum flavor. Taste and add sugar, if desired. Add the frozen pineapple to serve as ice cubes and keep the sangria cold. Ladle into punch cups.

SUNRISE SMOOTHIE

SERVES 3 OR 4

2 cups lemon yogurt	1 cup nonfat or low-fat milk
2 cups frozen raspberries	2 teaspoons vanilla extract

Process the yogurt, raspberries, milk and vanilla in a blender until smooth. Pour into serving glasses.

When the weather warms up, Chattanooga comes alive with the sound of music! Events include: Jazz Festival, a three-day springtime extravaganza; Pops on the River; and a July 4th celebration in Coolidge Park featuring Chattanooga's Symphony Orchestra. Miller Plaza is home to both the Nightfall Concert Series and the Rhythm & Noon Concert Series. The largest celebration of all is Riverbend—a nine-day, international award-winning festival held on the Tennessee Riverbank. Boasting performances from more than 100 bands, it's no wonder Chattanooga welcomes over 600,000 patrons to this event each year!

FRUITED MINT TEA

SERVES 10 TO 12

5 family-size tea bags
6 cups boiling water
1 1/2 cups sugar, or to taste
10 sprigs of fresh mint
2 cups cold water

1 (59- to 64-ounce) carton pure
premium orange juice
2/3 cup fresh lemon juice
1 (6-ounce) can pineapple juice
Fresh mint leaves for garnish

Steep the tea bags in the boiling water in a pitcher for 3 to 5 minutes. Remove the tea bags. Add the sugar and stir until dissolved. Place the mint sprigs in the cold water. Mash or bruise the mint to extract the flavor. Strain into the tea, discarding the solids. Let stand until cool. Add the orange juice, lemon juice and pineapple juice and mix well. Serve over crushed ice. Garnish with fresh mint leaves.

Photograph for this recipe appears on page 81.

"NADA" FRITTATA

SERVES 6

3/4 cup crushed ranch croutons
2 cups chopped tomatoes
2 cups (8 ounces) shredded
Colby-Jack cheese
3 tablespoons onion flakes
1 (2-ounce) can black olives
4 ounces feta cheese, crumbled

6 slices bacon, crisp-cooked and crumbled
5 eggs
1 cup whipping cream
1/8 teaspoon salt
1/4 teaspoon freshly ground pepper
1/8 teaspoon nutmeg

Spray a 10-inch quiche pan with nonstick cooking spray. Spread 1/4 cup of the crouton crumbs in the prepared pan. Layer 1 cup of the tomatoes, 1 cup of the Colby-Jack cheese, 1 1/2 tablespoons of the onion flakes and one-half of the olives over the crouton crumbs. Repeat the layers. Sprinkle the feta cheese and bacon over the layers. Combine the eggs, cream, salt, pepper and nutmeg in a bowl and mix well. Pour over the top. Sprinkle with the remaining 1/4 cup crouton crumbs. Bake in a preheated 325-degree oven for 45 to 50 minutes or until set. Let cool for 10 minutes before serving.

NOTE: This recipe was inspired by Pencarrow House, a five-star bed and breakfast in Queenstown, New Zealand.

GARDEN CLUB QUICHE

MAKES 1 DOZEN

3/4 (10-ounce) package frozen spinach
8 ounces bacon
1/2 cup finely chopped onion
16 ounces cottage cheese
6 ounces Swiss cheese, shredded

5 eggs, beaten
1 teaspoon Worcestershire sauce
Pepper to taste
Few drops of Tabasco sauce (optional)
1 ounce Parmesan cheese, grated (optional)

Cook the spinach using the package directions; drain. Squeeze out the excess liquid. Cook the bacon in a skillet until crisp. Remove the bacon to paper towels to drain, reserving the drippings in the skillet. Crumble the bacon. Sauté the onion in the reserved bacon drippings; drain.

Mash the cottage cheese with a potato masher in a large bowl until partially smooth. You may also use an immersion blender, if desired. Reserve 1/4 cup of the Swiss cheese and 1/4 cup of the bacon. Add the remaining bacon, the onion, eggs and remaining Swiss cheese to the cottage cheese and mix well. Add the Worcestershire sauce, pepper and Tabasco sauce and mix well. Divide the mixture equally among twelve greased muffin cups. Sprinkle each with 1 teaspoon each of the reserved bacon and Swiss cheese. Top evenly with the Parmesan cheese. Place the muffin pan on a baking sheet. Bake in a preheated 350-degree oven for 23 to 28 minutes or until a knife inserted in the centers come out clean. Do not overbake.

NOTE: This can also be made in a greased 10-inch pie plate. Bake for 35 to 40 minutes or until a knife inserted in the center comes out clean. Cool slightly before serving.

Established in 1931, the Junior League Garden Club of Chattanooga grew from the desire to "promote interest in horticulture, conservation, and related civic and cultural affairs" in harmony with the Junior League of Chattanooga. Monthly meetings involve a harvest of guest speakers with expertise in gardening, environmental preservation, the arts, and community issues. A service project is adopted annually, which has included plantings at the Children's Home/Chambliss Shelter, the courtyard at Girls Preparatory School, and St. Barnabas retirement community.

Amaretto Fruit Salad

Serves 6 to 8

1/2 cup amaretto
1/2 cup white wine
2 teaspoons fresh lemon juice
3 tablespoons sugar
1 bunch grapes, sliced

1 small honeydew melon, finely chopped
1 small pineapple, finely chopped
1 pint strawberries, sliced
1 large banana, sliced
1 sprig of fresh mint for garnish

Whisk the amaretto, wine, lemon juice and sugar together in a bowl until the sugar dissolves. Combine the grapes, melon, pineapple and strawberries in a large bowl. Pour the amaretto mixture over the top. Chill, covered, for 8 to 10 hours. Just before serving, stir in the banana. Garnish with the mint.

Note: Substitutions can be made with the fruit according to season and availability.

Blue Bandana Banana Bread

Makes 1 loaf

11/2 cups (3 sticks) butter or margarine, softened
1 cup sugar
2 eggs
1 teaspoon vanilla extract
11/2 cups all-purpose flour

1 teaspoon baking soda
1/4 teaspoon salt
2 ripe bananas, mashed
11/2 cups fresh, frozen or canned blueberries, drained
1/2 cup chopped nuts (optional)

Cream the butter and sugar in a mixing bowl until light and fluffy. Beat in the eggs and vanilla. Add the flour, baking soda and salt and mix well. Stir in the bananas, blueberries and nuts. Pour into a greased 5×9-inch loaf pan. Bake in a preheated 350-degree oven for 50 to 60 minutes or until the loaf tests done.

Baking Tip

Lightly coat chocolate chips, berries, etc. with flour before adding them to a bread or cake to prevent them from sinking to the bottom of the pan.

ZUCCHINI MUFFINS

MAKES ABOUT 2 DOZEN

3 eggs
2 cups all-purpose flour
2 cups sugar
1 cup rolled oats
1/2 cup vegetable oil
2 cups grated zucchini
1 tablespoon cinnamon
1 teaspoon baking soda
1 teaspoon salt
1 teaspoon vanilla extract
1 cup chopped pecans or walnuts

Beat the eggs in a mixing bowl until light. Add the flour, sugar, oats, oil, zucchini, cinnamon, baking soda, salt and vanilla and beat at low speed until mixed. Stir in the pecans. Pour into greased muffin cups. Bake in a preheated 350-degree oven for 20 to 25 minutes or until the muffins test done.

YUMMY BREAKFAST PASTRY

SERVES 8 TO 10

1 (12-count) can refrigerated original breadsticks
6 ounces cream cheese, softened
1 medium egg yolk
1/4 cup confectioners' sugar
3/4 cup blueberries
1 medium egg white
2 teaspoons water
1 cup confectioners' sugar
2 tablespoons orange juice

Unroll the breadstick dough lengthwise on a 10×15-inch baking pan lightly sprayed with nonstick cooking spray. Pinch the center seam of the dough to seal. Beat the cream cheese, egg yolk and confectioners' sugar in a mixing bowl until smooth. Spread down the center of the dough. Top with the blueberries. Starting at the top, bring each bread stick alternately toward the center in criss-cross fashion to cover the filling, braiding the dough all the way down. Brush with a mixture of the egg white and water. Bake in a preheated 375-degree oven for 20 minutes. Beat the confectioners' sugar and orange juice in a bowl until smooth. Spread over the pastry.

Photograph for this recipe appears at right.

A Brunch for Ladies Who Lunch

Fruited Mint Tea
Mimosas
Amaretto Fruit Salad
Absolutely Aspic
Garden Club Quiche
"Nada" Frittata
Heirloom Tomato and Walnut Pesto Pie
Yummy Breakfast Pastry

SUMMER SQUASH PASTA SOUP

SERVES 4

3 tablespoons butter
1 small onion, chopped
1 garlic clove, minced
3 small yellow squash, cut into halves lengthwise and thinly sliced
Sea salt and freshly ground pepper to taste
1/4 cup white wine
1 cup vegetable stock
2 cups chicken broth
2/3 cup ditalini pasta, or other short pasta
Juice of 1/2 large lemon
1/2 teaspoon chopped fresh thyme
1/4 teaspoon sea salt
1/4 teaspoon freshly ground pepper

Melt the butter in a large saucepan over medium-high heat. Add the onion and sauté for 3 minutes or until tender. Add the garlic and sauté just until fragrant. Add the squash and sauté for 3 minutes. Season with sea salt and pepper to taste. Add the wine. Cook until the wine is almost evaporated, stirring to scrape up the brown bits from the bottom of the saucepan. Add the stock and broth. Bring to a boil and add the pasta. Cook for 10 minutes or until al dente. Stir in the lemon juice, thyme, 1/4 teaspoon sea salt and 1/4 teaspoon pepper. Ladle into soup bowls.

Add a squeeze of lemon juice to a pot of any broth-based soup to "brighten" the flavor.

CREAM OF FRESH TOMATO SOUP

SERVES 6

3 tablespoons olive oil
2 small red onions, chopped
2 large carrots, chopped
4 garlic cloves, minced
6 large ripe tomatoes, coarsely chopped
1 1/2 teaspoons sugar
1 tablespoon tomato paste
1/4 cup packed chopped fresh basil leaves
3 cups rich chicken broth
1 tablespoon kosher salt
1 teaspoon freshly ground pepper
3/4 cup heavy cream
Julienned fresh basil leaves for garnish

Heat the olive oil in a large saucepan over medium heat. Add the onions and carrots. Sauté for 10 minutes or until tender. Add the garlic and cook for 1 minute. Add the tomatoes, sugar, tomato paste, chopped basil, broth, kosher salt and pepper and mix well. Bring to a boil. Reduce the heat and simmer, uncovered, for 30 to 40 minutes. Blend the soup to a smooth consistency with an immersion blender or process in batches in a food processor. Stir in the cream. Ladle into soup bowls. Garnish with julienned fresh basil.

69

Originally created by the Carter family as a private garden in an area known for its rocky terrain, Rock City as we now know it was opened to the public in 1932. Since then, travelers have been invited to explore this attraction with cries of "See Rock City" on more than nine hundred barns in nineteen states! Every season boasts new reasons to visit this Lookout Mountain destination, including views of seven states, fall corn mazes, and enchanted winter lights.

GAZPACHO

SERVES 8

2 slices dry white bread
2 tablespoons minced parsley
2 tablespoons fresh oregano
1/4 cup red wine vinegar
5 tablespoons olive oil
4 large tomatoes, coarsely chopped
2 red bell peppers, coarsely chopped
4 garlic cloves, minced
1 cup coarsely chopped red onion

1 cup coarsely chopped seeded cucumber
1/2 cup kalamata olives
1 (46-ounce) bottle tomato juice
1 tablespoon lemon juice
1 tablespoon Worcestershire sauce
4 teaspoons salt
1 teaspoon pepper
Hot pepper sauce to taste
Sour cream

Process the bread, parsley, oregano, vinegar and olive oil in a food processor until combined. Place in a large bowl. Add the tomatoes, bell peppers, garlic, onion, cucumber and olives and mix well. Stir in the tomato juice, lemon juice, Worcestershire sauce, salt, pepper and hot sauce. Chill, covered, for 3 hours to let the flavors combine. Ladle into soup bowls and dollop with sour cream.

ABSOLUTELY ASPIC

SERVES 16 TO 20

4 ribs celery, sliced
1 bell pepper, sliced
1 large onion, sliced
4 (16-ounce) cans whole tomatoes

1 teaspoon sugar
1 tablespoon vinegar
3 envelopes unflavored gelatin
1/2 cup cold water

Simmer the celery, bell pepper, onion, tomatoes, sugar and vinegar in a saucepan for 1 hour or until the vegetables are tender. Strain the broth into a large bowl, discarding the solids. Soften the gelatin in the cold water in a bowl. Add 1 cup of the hot broth and stir until the gelatin dissolves. Add the gelatin mixture to the remaining hot broth and mix well. Pour into an oiled 2-quart mold or bundt pan. Chill for 1 to 2 days or until set.

FROZEN CHAMPAGNE SALAD

SERVES 10 TO 12

8 ounces cream cheese, softened
1 cup sugar
12 ounces whipped topping
1 (15-ounce) can crushed pineapple, drained
1 (10-ounce) package frozen strawberries
1 cup chopped pecans
2 large bananas, sliced

Cream the cream cheese and sugar in a mixing bowl until light and fluffy. Fold in the whipped topping. Add the pineapple, undrained strawberries, pecans and bananas. Pour into a large mold sprayed with nonstick cooking spray or into a lightly greased 9×13-inch pan. Freeze for 4 to 10 hours or until firm. Remove from the freezer to soften for 10 minutes before serving. Invert onto a serving plate and serve.

BFT SANDWICHES

SERVES 4

1 cup crumbled good-quality feta cheese (4 ounces)
1/4 cup fresh basil chiffonade
1/4 cup low-fat mayonnaise
1/4 teaspoon freshly ground pepper
8 slices thinly sliced white bread or multigrain bread, toasted
8 (1/4-inch-thick) slices heirloom tomatoes

Combine the cheese, basil, mayonnaise and pepper in a bowl and toss with a fork to mix. Spread about 2 1/2 tablespoons of the cheese mixture onto each of four bread slices. Add two tomato slices to each and top with the remaining bread slices.

Photograph for this recipe appears on page 81.

Chiffonade (translated from a French phrase meaning, "made of rags") is a knife technique that involves slicing leafy vegetables or herbs into thin strips for a recipe or garnish. To cut a chiffonade, stack the leaves of the vegetable or herb (such as basil, spinach, or lettuce) largest to smallest, and then roll them tightly lengthwise on a cutting board. Use a sharp knife to cut slices off the roll. Fluff the shredded leaves with your fingers to help separate the slices before using.

BELOW THE LINE PIMENTO CHEESE

SERVES 6 TO 8

16 ounces sharp Cheddar cheese, coarsely shredded
16 ounces mild Cheddar cheese, coarsely shredded
8 ounces aged Parmesan cheese, grated
4 ounces cream cheese, softened
18 undrained green olives, minced
1 (2-ounce) jar chopped pimento, drained
1 teaspoon finely grated white onion
1/2 teaspoon minced garlic
2 teaspoons Worcestershire sauce
1 teaspoon Louisiana hot sauce
1/2 tablespoon freshly ground pepper
Juice of 1/2 lemon
1 cup (or more) mayonnaise
2 1/2 teaspoons sugar

Combine the sharp Cheddar cheese, mild Cheddar cheese, Parmesan cheese, cream cheese, olives, pimento, onion, garlic, Worcestershire sauce, hot sauce, pepper, lemon juice, mayonnaise and sugar in a large bowl and mix well. Serve as a sandwich spread, stuffed in tomatoes or as a twist on a BLT.

This recipe was woven over many years in the culinary-rich Mississippi Delta, and eventually wound its way over to the Scenic City. Now you can shred your own cheese or buy it already shredded. It is a labor of love, but it is much better shredded in your own kitchen. Also, almost all of the ingredients can be done to taste. But, this is a great start. If you ever need to bulk it up, add more mayonnaise. If it needs more spice, add more hot sauce or olives. And, if you want it to be less sweet, you can use less sugar.

SUSAN F. DAVENPORT'S STIR-FRIED FAJITAS

SERVES 4

2 garlic cloves, minced
2 teaspoons seasoned salt
2 teaspoons ground cumin
1 teaspoon chili powder
1 teaspoon crushed red pepper
3 tablespoons olive oil
3 tablespoons lemon juice
1 1/2 to 2 pounds beef or boneless skinless chicken, cut into strips

2 to 3 tablespoons vegetable oil
1 cup sliced onion
1 cup chopped green onions
1 cup sliced red or green bell pepper
8 flour tortillas, warmed
2 avocados, sliced
Sour cream
Salsa

Whisk the garlic, seasoned salt, cumin, chili powder, red pepper, olive oil and lemon juice together in a bowl. Add the beef and toss to coat. Marinate, covered, in the refrigerator for 2 hours or longer.

Heat the vegetable oil in a skillet over high heat. Add the sliced onion, green onions and bell pepper and stir-fry until light brown. Remove from the skillet and keep warm. Sauté the beef in the skillet for 4 minutes or until almost cooked through. Return the vegetables to the skillet. Stir-fry until heated through. Spoon into the tortillas and top with the avocados, sour cream and salsa.

Stir-Fried Fajitas is the recipe of the late Susan F. Davenport, one of our League's past presidents. More than just a great cook and devoted mother, Susan also was dedicated to philanthropic and volunteer efforts throughout our community. She served as president of both Family and Children's Services and the Community Foundation of Greater Chattanooga. Shortly after her passing, the League's annual Community Service Award was renamed in her memory. Then-president Caroline Bentley called Susan "the epitome of a volunteer—socially conscious, caring, compassionate, and hard working." Stir-Fried Fajitas remains a family favorite.

DRUNKEN BURGERS

SERVES 4

1 1/2 pounds ground chuck	1 tablespoon Dijon mustard
1 teaspoon salt	1 tablespoon minced fresh chives
1/2 teaspoon pepper	or shallot
1 1/2 tablespoons brandy	1 egg, lightly beaten

Crumble the ground chuck into a large bowl. Sprinkle with the salt and pepper. Mix the brandy, Dijon mustard, chives and egg in a bowl. Add to the ground chuck and mix lightly just until combined. Shape into four patties. Place on a grill rack or in a skillet. Grill or cook until the patties are cooked through, turning once.

NOTE: These burgers may also be served on a toasted French baguette. Adjust the patty size accordingly—make eight small patties and place two per person on 6-inch slices of bread. Or, slice the four patties into halves and arrange on the bread.

SLOW COOKIN' BARBECUED PORK

SERVES 10 TO 12

2 large onions, cut into quarters	1 teaspoon red pepper
2 tablespoons brown sugar	4 teaspoons Worcestershire sauce
1 tablespoon paprika	1 1/2 teaspoons sugar
2 teaspoons kosher salt	1 1/2 teaspoons dry mustard
1/2 teaspoon thyme	1/4 teaspoon garlic powder
1/2 teaspoon black pepper	1/4 teaspoon kosher salt
1 (4- to 6-pound) pork butt or	1/4 teaspoon cayenne pepper
picnic pork roast	1/2 teaspoon onion powder
2/3 cup cider vinegar	1/2 cup barbecue sauce, or more to taste
1 teaspoon liquid smoke	

Place the onions in a slow cooker. Mix the brown sugar, paprika, 2 teaspoons kosher salt, the thyme and black pepper together and rub into the pork. Place the pork on top of the onions. Whisk the vinegar, liquid smoke, red pepper, Worcestershire sauce, sugar, dry mustard, garlic powder, 1/4 teaspoon kosher salt, the cayenne pepper and onion powder together in a bowl. Pour over the pork. Cook on Low for 10 to 12 hours. Remove all but about 1/2 cup of the drippings from the slow cooker. Stir in the barbecue sauce. Cook for 30 minutes longer.

NOTE: Tennessee Whiskey Barbecue Sauce on page 86 may be used in this recipe.

74

SAUSAGE-STUFFED HEIRLOOM TOMATOES
SERVES 6 TO 12

6 to 12 heirloom tomatoes
Salt and freshly ground black pepper to taste
2 tablespoons olive oil
1 yellow onion, finely chopped
8 ounces cremini mushrooms, finely chopped
3 garlic cloves, finely chopped
1 pound mild Italian sausage, casings removed
1/4 teaspoon red pepper flakes
1 teaspoon minced fresh oregano
2 cups lightly toasted bread crumbs
1/4 cup minced fresh Italian parsley
3/4 cup (3 ounces) freshly grated Parmesan cheese
Olive oil

Core the tomatoes using a paring knife. Scoop out the pulp with a spoon. Sprinkle the inside of each tomato with salt and black pepper. Place cut side down on a plate to drain.

Heat 2 tablespoons olive oil in a sauté pan over medium-high heat. Add the onion and cook for 5 minutes. Add the mushrooms, salt and black pepper and cook for 5 minutes. Add the garlic and cook for 1 minute. Add the sausage and red pepper flakes. Cook for 3 to 5 minutes or until cooked through, stirring to break up the sausage into small pieces. Remove to a bowl to cool for 10 minutes. Stir the oregano, bread crumbs, parsley and 1/2 cup of the cheese into the sausage mixture. Spoon into the tomatoes and place in a baking dish. Sprinkle the remaining 1/4 cup cheese evenly over the tomatoes. Drizzle with olive oil. Bake in a preheated 375-degree oven for 30 to 35 minutes or until heated through. Let stand for 5 minutes before serving.

This stuffing can also be used to stuff bell peppers, eggplant, or summer squash. Scoop the pulp out of the eggplant or squash and replace with the stuffing mixture. The baking time will be longer if eggplant is used. Save the pulp from the tomatoes and make Heirloom Salsa Verde on page 19.

Signature "Fried" Chicken

Serves 4

1/2 cup salt
1/4 cup sugar
2 tablespoons paprika
2 large heads garlic, cloves separated and crushed
3 bay leaves
2 sprigs of fresh rosemary
7 cups buttermilk
2 1/2 tablespoons Sriracha hot chile sauce
1 (3- to 4-pound) chicken, cut into 8 pieces
2 eggs
1 1/2 tablespoons Dijon mustard
1 teaspoon dried thyme
1 teaspoon salt
1/2 teaspoon black pepper
1/2 teaspoon dried oregano
1/2 teaspoon garlic powder
1/2 teaspoon paprika
1/2 teaspoon rubbed sage
1/2 teaspoon onion powder
1/4 teaspoon cayenne pepper
1 (5-ounce) package Melba Toast, crushed
1/4 cup vegetable oil

Combine 1/2 cup salt, the sugar, 2 tablespoons paprika, the garlic, bay leaves, rosemary, buttermilk and hot chile sauce in a bowl and mix until the salt and sugar are dissolved. Place the chicken in a large sealable plastic bag. Add the buttermilk mixture and seal the bag. Marinate in the refrigerator for 2 to 3 hours. Remove the chicken from the buttermilk mixture, shaking off the excess. Place in a single layer on a wire rack over a baking sheet. Chill, uncovered, for 2 hours.

Place the oven rack in the upper middle position. Cover a rimmed baking sheet with foil and set a wire rack over it. Mix the eggs, Dijon mustard, thyme, 1 teaspoon salt, the black pepper, oregano, garlic powder, 1/2 teaspoon paprika, the sage, onion powder and cayenne pepper together in a shallow dish. Combine the Melba toast and oil in a shallow dish and mix well. Coat the chicken on both sides with the egg mixture. Dredge in the Melba toast mixture, pressing the crumbs to coat both sides. Shake off any excess and place the chicken in a single layer on the wire rack. Bake in a preheated 400-degree oven for 40 to 50 minutes or until cooked through.

PANKO CRUMB CHICKEN

SERVES 8

8 boneless skinless chicken breasts
2 cups (4 sticks) butter, melted
2 cups panko (Japanese bread crumbs)
3/4 cup (3 ounces) grated Parmesan cheese
1/4 cup chopped fresh parsley
2 garlic cloves, pressed
2 teaspoons salt
1/2 teaspoon pepper

Soak the chicken in the butter in a bowl for 3 minutes on each side. Mix the bread crumbs, cheese, parsley, garlic, salt and pepper in a large bowl. Remove the chicken from the butter and dredge in the panko mixture to coat, reserving the butter. Place in a single layer in a 9×13-inch baking dish. Pour the reserved butter over the top. Bake in a preheated 350-degree oven for 30 minutes or until brown and cooked through.

The Scenic City has a reputation for outdoor recreation and environmental conservation. On dry land, adventures include camping, cycling, rock climbing, and cave exploration. If you don't mind getting wet, kayak or raft the Ocoee River's Class III and IV rapids, home of the 1996 Olympic Whitewater Competitions. To enjoy a more relaxed ride, follow the Tennessee River Blueway, a fifty-mile mapped-out trip for paddlers. To appreciate some of the city's best views, take a flying leap off Lookout Mountain at the largest hang-gliding school in the country, Lookout Mountain Flight School.

BASIL-INFUSED SCALLOPS

SERVES 4

1/2 cup fresh basil, minced
1 garlic clove, minced
1 tablespoon extra-virgin olive oil
1/2 teaspoon kosher salt
1/4 teaspoon freshly ground pepper
1 1/2 pounds large (preferably dry) sea scallops, small side muscle removed
1 or 2 pinches of kosher salt
1 or 2 pinches of freshly ground pepper
2 tablespoons vegetable oil
2 tablespoons unsalted butter
Lemon wedges for garnish

Mix the basil, garlic, olive oil, 1/2 teaspoon kosher salt and 1/4 teaspoon pepper together on a cutting board, by repeatedly chopping and spreading with the flat blade of a knife until almost a puréed consistency.

Dry the scallops in a single layer between several sheets of paper towels by pressing and blotting gently. Sprinkle 1 or 2 pinches of kosher salt and 1 or 2 pinches of pepper on each side. Cut a horizontal slit about three-quarters of the way through each scallop. Open carefully, spoon about 1/2 teaspoon of the basil mixture into each scallop and then close.

Heat 1 tablespoon of the vegetable oil in a large nonstick skillet over high heat until shimmering and almost smoking. Place one-half of the scallops in the hot oil in a single layer without the sides touching. Cook until brown. Add 1 tablespoon of the butter to the skillet. Turn the scallops and baste with the pan drippings. Cook for 1 minute or until the scallops are opaque and firm. Remove to a warmed platter to keep warm. Wipe out the skillet with a paper towel and repeat the process with the remaining vegetable oil, scallops and butter. Garnish with lemon wedges and serve immediately.

NOTE: These can also be grilled. Brush a couple tablespoons of vegetable oil on each side of the scallops before placing on a grill rack. Grill over high heat for 8 minutes or until seared on each side.

If you can only find wet (phosphate-treated) scallops, soak them in a mixture of 4 cups cold water, 1/4 cup fresh lemon juice, and 2 tablespoons salt for 30 minutes. Dry the scallops on paper towels before cooking. Don't add the salt called for in the recipe.

PAN-SEARED SALMON WITH DILL CREAM SAUCE

SERVES 4

DILL CREAM SAUCE
1/2 cup mayonnaise
1/2 cup sour cream
1 small shallot, minced
3 tablespoons minced fresh parsley leaves
2 tablespoons Dijon mustard
2 tablespoons minced fresh dill weed
2 teaspoons fresh lemon juice
1 teaspoon horseradish (optional)
Salt and pepper to taste

SALMON
2 tablespoons extra-virgin olive oil
4 salmon fillets
Pinch of salt
Pinch of pepper

To prepare the sauce, combine the mayonnaise, sour cream, shallot, parsley, Dijon mustard, dill weed, lemon juice, horseradish, salt and pepper in a bowl and mix well. Spoon into an airtight container. Chill for 1 hour or up to 3 days.

To prepare the salmon, heat the olive oil in a large skillet over medium heat until hot and shiny, tilting the skillet to make sure the bottom is coated. Place the salmon skin side down in the hot oil. Sprinkle with salt and pepper. Cook for 5 minutes or until the skin is brown. Turn the salmon carefully. Cook for 3 minutes or until firm and cooked through. Serve with the sauce on the top or on the side.

GRILLED SNAPPER WITH CAPERS AND DILL

SERVES 4

4 (4- to 6-ounce) snapper fillets
1/4 cup olive oil
Pinch each of salt and pepper
1/4 cup minced garlic
1/4 cup chopped fresh dill weed
1/4 cup capers

Place the fish on a grilling rack designed for grilling seafood. Drizzle evenly with the olive oil. Sprinkle with the salt and pepper. Spread the garlic, dill weed and capers over the top. Grill in a preheated 180- to 200-degree grill for 25 to 30 minutes or until the fish flakes easily.

For perfect charcoal grilling, wait until coals are ashy or burning embers. If you can hold your hand close to the grill for about four seconds, the temperature is "medium" and will cook your meat more evenly. An open flame is actually cooler than ashy embers and will result in unevenly cooked food.

SUMMERTIME BRIE PASTA

SERVES 4 TO 6

4 large ripe tomatoes, peeled, seeded and cut into 1/2-inch pieces
1 pound Brie cheese, rind removed and cheese torn into pieces
1 cup fresh basil, cut into strips
3 garlic cloves, minced
1 cup extra-virgin olive oil
1/2 teaspoon salt
1/2 teaspoon freshly ground pepper
6 quarts (24 cups) water
1 tablespoon extra-virgin olive oil
1 teaspoon salt
1 1/2 pounds linguini
1 cup freshly grated Parmesan cheese, or to taste

Combine the tomatoes, Brie cheese, basil, garlic, 1 cup olive oil, 1/2 teaspoon salt and the pepper in a large bowl and mix well. Let stand at room temperature for 2 to 4 hours before serving.

Bring the water to a boil in a large saucepan. Add 1 tablespoon olive oil, 1 teaspoon salt and the pasta. Boil for 8 to 10 minutes or until the pasta is al dente; drain. Add the pasta to the tomato mixture and toss to coat. Sprinkle with Parmesan cheese.

DEVIL IN DISGUISE EGGS

MAKES 2 DOZEN

1 dozen eggs	1 teaspoon fresh lemon juice
1/4 cup mayonnaise	1/4 teaspoon cayenne pepper
1/4 cup Dijon mustard	Salt and white pepper to taste
1/4 cup (1/2 stick) butter, softened	Paprika

Place the eggs in a large saucepan and cover with cold water. Bring to a boil. Cover and turn off the heat. Let stand for 15 minutes; drain. Run cold water over the eggs until completely cool.

Peel the eggs and cut into halves lengthwise. Remove the yolks and rub through a fine mesh strainer into a bowl. Add the mayonnaise, Dijon mustard and butter and mix until smooth. Stir in the lemon juice and cayenne pepper. Season with salt and white pepper. Be sure to season well as the flavors dull when the eggs are chilled. Spoon into a pastry bag fitted with a star tip or into a plastic bag with the corner snipped. Pipe the yolk mixture into the egg whites. Sprinkle with paprika. Chill until serving time.

CHEESY ZUCCHINI CASSEROLE

SERVES 6

2 tablespoons olive oil	1/2 cup sour cream
2 tablespoons butter	2 pinches of salt
6 cups sliced zucchini	2 pinches of pepper
1 Vidalia onion, finely chopped	1 cup (4 ounces) shredded Cheddar cheese
1 garlic clove, minced	1 cup crushed potato chips

Heat 1 tablespoon of the olive oil and 1 tablespoon of the butter in a large skillet over medium-high heat. Add the zucchini. Cook for 10 to 15 minutes or until the zucchini begins to soften. Remove the zucchini to a plate lined with paper towels. Add the remaining 1 tablespoon olive oil and 1 tablespoon butter in the skillet. Add the onion. Cook for 8 to 10 minutes or until the onion begins to soften. Add the garlic. Cook for 3 minutes or until soft. Turn off the heat. Stir in the sour cream, salt and pepper.

Place paper towels over the zucchini and press to remove any excess moisture. Layer the onion mixture, one-half of the cheese, the zucchini and remaining cheese in a buttered 9×9-inch baking dish. Bake, covered with foil, in a preheated 350-degree oven for 25 minutes. Remove the foil. Top with the potato chips. Bake for 5 minutes longer or until brown, watching carefully to prevent overbrowning. Let stand for 10 minutes before serving.

Freeze blocks of cheese for about ten minutes before hand grating them. The cheese will be firmer and stay colder longer, making it easier to grate.

Heirloom Tomato And Walnut Pesto Pie

Serves 4 to 6

2 cups packed fresh basil leaves
1/4 cup toasted walnuts
1 garlic clove, crushed
1/2 teaspoon kosher salt
1/4 teaspoon freshly ground pepper
1/2 to 3/4 cup good-quality extra-virgin olive oil
1/2 cup (2 ounces) grated Parmesan cheese
Kosher salt and pepper to taste
1 baked (9-inch) pie shell, cooled
1 1/2 pounds ripe heirloom tomatoes, cut into 1/8-inch-thick slices
2 tablespoons basil chiffonade for garnish
Good-quality extra-virgin olive oil

Pulse 2 cups basil, the walnuts, garlic, 1/2 teaspoon kosher salt and 1/4 teaspoon pepper in a blender or food processor fifteen to twenty times or until finely chopped. Add 1/2 to 3/4 cup olive oil gradually until the mixture becomes smooth and thick, processing constantly. Add the cheese and pulse ten more times or until mixed. Season with kosher salt and pepper to taste and pulse again. Spread the pesto over the cooled pie shell using a spatula. Arrange the tomatoes in a circular pattern over the pesto. Garnish with the basil chiffonade. Drizzle with olive oil and sprinkle with kosher salt and pepper to taste. Cut into wedges to serve.

NOTE: For more interest and a prettier dish, choose different colored tomatoes, such as yellow and purple. Do not use green tomatoes. Alternate the colors of tomatoes when arranging in the pie shell.

Picnic spots abound at Coolidge Park, twenty-two acres located on the Tennessee River's North Shore. Cool off in the fountains, but watch out for sculpted lions, camels, and elephants, oh my! They spray water at random! After drying off, grab an ice cream and go rock climbing. If you prefer, hop onto the historic hand-carved, hand-painted Dentzel carousel, complete with a calliope band organ. Commissioned in Philadelphia in 1895, the carousel was retired from Grant Park in Atlanta and brought to Chattanooga, where it was restored by a local master woodcarver.

AUNT BECKY'S GARLIC PICKLES

MAKES 2 QUARTS

1/2 gallon kosher dill pickles
4 cups (scant) sugar
14 garlic cloves
1 tablespoon pickling spices
1 cup vinegar

Cut the pickles into 1/2-inch slices and place in a large bowl. Add the sugar, garlic and spices. Bring the vinegar to a boil in a saucepan. Pour over the pickles. Let stand, covered, for 4 to 5 days, stirring each day to keep the seasoning well mixed. Pack into sterilized jars, leaving 1/4 inch headspace. Seal with two-piece lids. Store in the refrigerator.

NOTE: This pickle is great with country ham and turkey during the holidays or on ham and turkey sandwiches. Use the juice to perk up deviled eggs and homemade pimento cheese.

EIGHT-BEER RUB

MAKES ABOUT 7 1/4 CUPS

1 (1-pound) package dark brown sugar
3/4 cup paprika
3/4 cup garlic powder
1/2 cup chili powder
1/2 cup black pepper
1/2 cup salt
1/2 cup cinnamon
1/2 cup onion powder
1/4 cup dry mustard
2 tablespoons dried basil
1 tablespoon cayenne pepper
1 teaspoon (heaping) ground cloves
1 teaspoon (heaping) nutmeg

Mix the brown sugar, paprika, garlic powder, chili powder, black pepper, salt, cinnamon, onion powder, dry mustard, basil, cayenne pepper, cloves and nutmeg in a large bowl. Use as a dry rub on meat, poultry, game, ribs, etc. Do not use barbecue sauce with this rub at any time while cooking.

NOTE: Legend has it this recipe was created over the course of eight beers.

PRESTO PESTO

MAKES ABOUT 3 1/4 CUPS

1 cup packed fresh spinach
1/2 cup fresh parsley
1/2 cup fresh basil
2 garlic cloves
1/4 cup walnuts
1/2 cup (2 ounces) shredded Parmesan cheese
Salt and pepper to taste
1/2 cup extra-virgin olive oil

Process the spinach, parsley, basil, garlic, walnuts, cheese, salt and pepper in a food processor until blended. Add the olive oil gradually in a fine stream, processing constantly until smooth. Serve over hot cooked pasta.

RÉMOULADE SAUCE

MAKES 1 PINT

1/4 cup lemon juice
1/4 cup vinegar
1/4 cup whole-grain mustard
1/4 cup horseradish
2 tablespoons salt
1/2 teaspoon black pepper
2 teaspoons paprika
Dash of cayenne pepper
1/2 cup chopped celery
1/2 cup chopped green onions
1/4 cup mayonnaise
1 cup vegetable oil

Blend the lemon juice, vinegar, mustard, horseradish, salt, black pepper, paprika, cayenne pepper, celery, green onions and mayonnaise in a blender for several minutes. Add the oil gradually, processing constantly until emulsified.

TENNESSEE WHISKEY BARBECUE SAUCE

MAKES ABOUT 3 1/2 CUPS

2 to 3 tablespoons vegetable oil
1 onion, minced
1 (8-ounce) can tomato sauce
1 (28-ounce) can whole tomatoes
3/4 cup distilled white vinegar
1/2 cup Tennessee whiskey or bourbon
1/4 cup firmly packed dark brown sugar
2 tablespoons molasses

1 tablespoon sweet paprika
1 tablespoon chili powder
2 teaspoons liquid smoke
2 teaspoons salt
2 teaspoons black pepper
1 teaspoon dry mustard
1 teaspoon Worcestershire sauce
1/4 cup orange juice

Heat the oil in a large saucepan over medium heat. Add the onion and sauté for 10 minutes or until the onion is soft and beginning to brown. Add the tomato sauce, undrained tomatoes, vinegar, whiskey, brown sugar, molasses, paprika, chili powder, liquid smoke, salt, black pepper, dry mustard, Worcestershire sauce and orange juice and mix well. Bring to a boil. Reduce the heat as low as possible. Simmer, uncovered, for 2 to 2 1/2 hours or until thick. Purée with an immersion blender until smooth. Store in an airtight container in the refrigerator for up to 2 weeks or in the freezer for up to 4 months.

NOTE: We stay true to our Tennessee roots and use Jack Daniel's® Tennessee Whiskey for this recipe.

RED WINE AND BLUEBERRY SAUCE

MAKES ABOUT 3 CUPS

1/2 cup water
1/2 cup sugar
1/2 cup dry red wine
3 tablespoons fresh lemon juice

1 1/2 tablespoons cornstarch
1 to 1 1/2 cups fresh blueberries
1/4 teaspoon cinnamon
1/8 teaspoon nutmeg

Combine the water, sugar, wine, lemon juice and cornstarch in a medium saucepan. Cook over medium heat until the cornstarch dissolves and the mixture comes to a boil, stirring constantly. Add the blueberries. Boil for 5 minutes or until the sauce thickens and coats the back of a spoon, stirring constantly. Remove from the heat and cool for 10 minutes. Stir in the cinnamon and nutmeg. Purée with an immersion blender, if desired.

NOTE: Try this served over lemon ice cream or pound cake.

SOUTHERN STAR'S BANANA PUDDING

SERVES 8

3 cups milk
1/4 cup (1/2 stick) butter
1 cup sugar
3 tablespoons cornstarch
3 tablespoons water
3 egg yolks
1 1/2 tablespoons vanilla extract
4 large ripe bananas, sliced
1/2 (12-ounce) package vanilla wafers
3 egg whites, at room temperature
3/4 cup sugar
1/2 teaspoon cream of tartar

Combine the milk, butter and 1 cup sugar in a heavy saucepan and mix well. Cook until the sugar is dissolved and the mixture is simmering, stirring occasionally. Stir the cornstarch into the water in a small bowl. Stir into the milk mixture. Cook until thickened, stirring constantly. Whisk the egg yolks lightly in a bowl. Add about 1 cup of the hot mixture 2 tablespoonfuls at a time to the egg yolks. Stir the egg yolks into the hot mixture. Remove from the heat. Stir in the vanilla.

Alternate layers of the bananas, vanilla wafers and custard in a greased 2-quart baking dish until all of the ingredients are used, ending with the custard. Beat the egg whites at high speed in a mixing bowl until soft peaks form. Add 3/4 cup sugar and the cream of tartar gradually, beating constantly until stiff peaks form. Dollop the meringue over the top of the pudding and spread evenly, sealing the meringue to the edges. Bake in a preheated 350-degree for 6 to 8 minutes or until light brown.

The Southern Star took shape from the shared vision of Rick and Nancy Adams for a restaurant coupling tasteful, fresh-daily dishes with an emphasis on Southern cuisine and a welcoming hospitality to match. The Star opened in October of 2000 in Chattanooga's Southside district and became a city-wide favorite practically overnight.

BANANA SPLIT PIE

SERVES 8 TO 10

3 cups crushed vanilla wafers
1/4 cup (1/2 stick) butter, melted
2 cups confectioners' sugar
1/2 cup (1 stick) butter, softened
2 eggs
5 bananas, cut into slices lengthwise
1 (11-ounce) can crushed pineapple
16 ounces whipped topping
1 cup chopped pecans
1/2 (10-ounce) jar maraschino cherries for garnish

Mix the vanilla wafer crumbs with 1/4 cup butter in a bowl. Press over the bottom of a 9×13-inch dish. Combine the confectioners' sugar, 1/2 cup butter and the eggs in a mixing bowl and beat for 10 minutes. Do not underbeat. Spread over the crust. Layer the bananas and then the pineapple over the confectioners' sugar mixture. Spread the whipped topping over the top. Sprinkle with the pecans. Garnish with the maraschino cherries. Store in the refrigerator.

NOTE: If you are concerned about using raw eggs, use eggs pasteurized in their shells, which are sold at some specialty food stores, or use an equivalent amount of pasteurized egg substitute.

CREAMY LEMONADE PIE
SERVES 8 TO 10

2 (5-ounce) cans evaporated milk
2 (4-ounce) packages lemon instant pudding mix
22 ounces cream cheese, softened
1 (12-ounce) can frozen lemonade concentrate, partially thawed
1 (9-ounce) graham cracker pie shell
Whipped cream for garnish
Sprigs of fresh mint for garnish
Lemon slices for garnish

Whisk the evaporated milk and pudding mix in a bowl for 2 minutes or until thickened. Place the cream cheese in the bowl of a stand mixer fitted with the whisk attachment. Beat at medium speed until fluffy. Add the lemonade concentrate and beat until blended. Beat in the pudding mixture until blended. Pour into the pie shell. Freeze for 4 hours or until firm. Garnish with whipped cream, sprigs of fresh mint and lemon slices.

Photograph for this recipe appears on page 55.

There's a reason the term "cherry on top of the sundae" is used so often—never underestimate the power of a garnish! Using items you already have in your kitchen can spruce up any weeknight meal or make the presentation of a special dish even more impressive. For example, keep some chocolate syrup, canned whipped cream, confectioners' sugar, baking cocoa, nuts, and berries handy when plating sweets such as cakes, pies, bread puddings, pancakes, and waffles. Nuts, berries, wedges of cheese, and snips of fresh herbs can liven up meats, entrées, and egg dishes.

SLOPPY PINEAPPLE CAKE
SERVES 10 TO 12

CAKE
2 cups all-purpose flour
2 teaspoons baking soda
2 cups sugar
1 (20-ounce) can crushed pineapple
2 eggs

VANILLA ICING
3/4 cup evaporated milk
1/2 cup (1 stick) butter
1 cup sugar
1 teaspoon vanilla extract

To prepare the cake, mix the flour and baking soda together. Combine the sugar, pineapple and eggs in a bowl and mix well. Add the flour mixture and mix well. Pour into a greased 9×13-inch cake pan. Bake in a preheated 350-degree oven for 30 to 40 minutes or until set and golden brown.

To prepare the icing, bring the evaporated milk, butter, sugar and vanilla to a boil in a saucepan. Cook for 5 minutes, stirring constantly. Prick holes in the warm cake. Pour the icing over the top.

To ensure an evenly baked cake, be sure all ingredients are at room temperature when beginning to prepare.

Caramelitas

Makes 2 dozen

1 cup all-purpose flour
1 cup quick-cooking oats
3/4 cup firmly packed brown sugar
1/2 teaspoon baking soda
1/4 teaspoon salt
3/4 cup (11/2 sticks) butter, melted
1 cup (6 ounces) semisweet chocolate chips
1/2 cup chopped pecans
3/4 cup caramel ice cream topping
3 tablespoons all-purpose flour

Mix 1 cup flour, the oats, brown sugar, baking soda, salt and butter in a large bowl until crumbly. Press one-half of the oat mixture over the bottom of a 7×11-inch baking pan. Bake in a preheated 350-degree oven for 10 minutes. Remove from the oven and maintain the oven temperature. Sprinkle with the chocolate chips and pecans. Blend the ice cream topping with 3 tablespoons flour and drizzle over the top. Sprinkle with the remaining oat mixture. Bake for 15 to 20 minutes or until golden brown. Chill or freeze until serving time. If frozen, remove from the freezer 1 hour before cutting into bars.

Catch the future stars of Major League Baseball right here in Chattanooga! Named for iconic Lookout Mountain, the Lookouts have been a part of the Scenic City's landscape for more than one hundred years. Located in the heart of downtown on historic Hawk Hill, AT&T Field serves as the home of the class AA Lookouts, affiliate of the Los Angeles Dodgers. The birthplace of some famous heavy hitters, a night with the Lookouts provides affordable family entertainment…a home-run in our book!

RAZZLE DAZZLE BARS

MAKES 2 DOZEN

1 cup pecans, coarsely chopped
1 1/2 cups all-purpose flour
1 1/4 cups old-fashioned rolled oats
1/3 cup granulated sugar
1/3 cup packed dark brown sugar
1 teaspoon kosher salt
1/2 tablespoon baking soda
3/4 cup (1 1/2 sticks) butter, melted
1 1/2 cups raspberry preserves

Butter an 8×8-inch baking pan. Line the bottom and sides with baking parchment. Spread the pecans in a baking dish. Bake in a preheated 350-degree oven for 5 minutes or until light brown and fragrant. Remove from the oven to cool. Maintain the oven temperature.

Whisk the flour, oats, granulated sugar, brown sugar, kosher salt, baking soda and toasted pecans in a large bowl. Add the butter and stir with a wooden spoon to mix well. Press two-thirds of the oat mixture in an even layer over the bottom of the prepared pan. Spread with the preserves. Sprinkle the remaining oat mixture over the top. Bake for 45 minutes or until the top is golden brown, rotating the pan halfway through baking. Cool in the pan on a wire rack for 3 hours. Cut into bars.

Schools in Hamilton County have been recipients of the League's support for more than fifty years. Historically, the League has subsidized teacher salaries, purchased books and supplies, and provided transportation for school children throughout the city. Supported institutions include Scenic Land School, Orange Grove School, and Siskin Children's Institute. Today the League awards more than $20,000 annually to Hamilton County public school teachers through our Mini-Grants program, which directly impacts the lives of our community's children.

COWBOY COOKIES

MAKES 5 DOZEN

2 cups all-purpose flour	1 cup granulated sugar
1 teaspoon baking soda	2 eggs
1 teaspoon baking powder	2 teaspoons vanilla extract
1 teaspoon salt	2 cups (12 ounces) chocolate chips
1 cup shortening	2 cups quick-cooking oats
1 cup dark brown sugar	1/2 cup nuts (optional)

Sift the flour, baking soda, baking powder and salt together. Cream the shortening, brown sugar and granulated sugar in a mixing bowl until fluffy. Add the eggs and vanilla and beat well. Add the flour mixture and mix well. Stir in the chocolate chips, oats and nuts. Roll the dough into small balls and place 2 inches apart on a greased cookie sheet. Dip the bottom of a glass in water and press the dough balls until flattened to 3/8 inch thick. Bake in a preheated 350-degree oven for 12 to 15 minutes or until golden brown. Cool on a wire rack. Store in an airtight container.

POTATO CHIP COOKIES

MAKES 3 TO 4 DOZEN

1 cup (2 sticks) butter, softened	1 cup crushed potato chips
3/4 cup granulated sugar	1 cup chopped pecans
11/2 cups all-purpose flour	1 cup confectioners' sugar
1 teaspoon vanilla extract	

Cream the butter and granulated sugar in a mixing bowl until light and fluffy. Add the flour gradually, beating well after each addition. Add the vanilla and potato chips and mix well. Fold in the pecans. Drop by small spoonfuls onto an ungreased cookie sheet. Dip the bottom of a glass in the confectioners' sugar and press the cookies to flatten. Bake in a preheated 350-degree oven for 8 to 10 minutes or until golden brown. Cool on a wire rack.

A Season of Comfort

As the leaves change to deep russet, gold, and orange, the mountains of East Tennessee come alive with activity. By foot, bike, or boat, many Chattanoogans would count fall as their favorite season to explore our region thanks to cooler temperatures and breathtaking scenery. An adventure is never far away on one of the region's many hiking trails, including portions of the Cumberland Trail and various routes on Lookout, Signal and Raccoon mountains. With destinations such as Lover's Leap and Sunset Rock, it's not hard to see why folks love to experience the great outdoors in Chattanooga. Farther afield, Fall Creek Falls State Park is home to the highest waterfall in the eastern United States, making it a popular spot to squeeze in one last camping trip before the weather turns cold.

Winding through the heart of downtown, the Tennessee River provides another vantage point to enjoy the splendor of fall in the Scenic City. For a slow, relaxing afternoon, a fall color cruise through the Tennessee River Gorge is a beautiful way to sightsee; those who prefer more action can cheer on teams at the Head of the Hooch rowing regatta, which has been contested in our area for thirty years. With cooler temperatures also come the perennial Southern favorites of tailgating and cheering on our favorite teams. Be they Mocs, Bulldogs, Volunteers, or Titans, we are reminded of the values of hospitality and tradition as we gather with old friends and strangers alike.

Families spend lazy fall weekends together exploring local apple orchards and sipping homemade cider, picking out the perfect pumpkins and gourds, or navigating a giant corn maze. Each of these gatherings reminds us to give thanks for our blessings, each other, and the bounty of our region.

Autumn

Autumn

Dinner After the Hayride

Point Park Punch
Baked Brie en Croûte
Shrimp de Jonghe
Curried Pumpkin Bisque
Sweet Pecan and Apple Salad
Easy-Peasey Skillet Mac and Cheesy
Bourbon Roast
Trick-or-Treat Bread
Bread Pudding with Jack Daniel's® Sauce

SHRIMP DE JONGHE

SERVES 8

10 tablespoons butter
2 cups fresh bread crumbs
3 tablespoons minced fresh flat-leaf parsley
1/2 teaspoon kosher salt
1/4 teaspoon freshly ground pepper
1 tablespoon dried basil
1/2 cup (2 ounces) freshly grated Parmesan cheese
5 garlic cloves, minced
1 1/2 pounds uncooked shrimp, peeled and deveined
1/2 cup dry white wine
1 French baguette, sliced

Melt the butter in a large skillet over medium-high heat. Add the bread crumbs. Heat until the bread crumbs have absorbed the butter, stirring constantly. Remove from the heat. Add the parsley, kosher salt, pepper, basil, cheese and garlic and mix well.

Spread one-half of the bread crumb mixture in an even layer in a buttered heavy 3-quart baking dish. Arrange the shrimp in a single layer over the bread crumb mixture. Spread the remaining bread crumb mixture evenly over the shrimp. Drizzle the wine over the top. Bake in a preheated 450-degree oven for 20 minutes or until brown and bubbly. Serve immediately with the bread on the side.

Shrimp can be purchased already peeled, deveined, and with tails removed in a package in the frozen food section. To thaw, place the package in the refrigerator the day before using. Rinse the shrimp and pat dry before adding to the dish. To thaw quickly, place the shrimp in a colander in the sink and run cool water over them until no longer frozen; pat dry.

HAIR OF THE DOG PUB SHROOMIES

SERVES 6

1 pound uncooked bratwurst
1/2 cup water
1/3 cup bleu cheese crumbles
1 tablespoon Worcestershire sauce
1/3 cup mayonnaise
1/3 teaspoon finely ground pepper
1/3 cup finely chopped onion
1/3 cup finely chopped green bell pepper
3 tablespoons jarred minced garlic in oil
2 tablespoons butter
15 to 20 button mushrooms

Remove the bratwurst from the casing. Sauté the bratwurst with the water in a skillet over medium-high heat until brown. Drain in a colander. Beat the bratwurst in a large bowl with a whisk until separated. Add the cheese, Worcestershire sauce, mayonnaise and pepper and mix well. Sauté the onion, bell pepper and garlic in the butter in a skillet until softened. Add to the bratwurst mixture and mix well.

Clean the mushrooms by brushing with a soft bristled brush or wiping with a damp kitchen towel. Remove and discard the stems or reserve for another purpose. Fill the mushroom caps with the bratwurst mixture to slightly overflowing. Place in a glass baking dish. Bake, uncovered, in a preheated 350-degree oven for 15 to 20 minutes or until heated through.

Hair of the Dog Pub, which opened in 2005, is a vision of an old world English pub and local watering hole with neighborhood charm. Travelers and locals alike feel at home here and enjoy meals that combine comfort food and unique pub-style cuisine that keep customers coming back.

SMOKEY'S SAUSAGE CUPS

SERVES 20

1 pound spicy bulk pork sausage
8 ounces cream cheese, softened
1 bunch green onions, chopped
3 (15-count) packages phyllo cups

Brown the sausage in a skillet, stirring until crumbly. Drain and let cool slightly. Combine the sausage, cream cheese and green onions in a bowl and mix well. Spoon into the phyllo cups and place on a baking sheet. Bake in a preheated 350-degree oven for 15 minutes or until heated through.

NOTE: The sausage filling can be made ahead of time and stored in the refrigerator until serving time.

Photograph for this recipe appears at right.

HALLELUJAH HAM LOAVES

MAKES 5 DOZEN

1 cup (2 sticks) butter, softened
3 tablespoons poppy seeds
3 tablespoons mustard
1 teaspoon Worcestershire sauce
1 onion, minced
1 pound cooked boneless ham, minced
12 ounces Swiss cheese, shredded
60 small party rolls

Beat the butter, poppy seeds, mustard and Worcestershire sauce in a bowl until creamy. Add the onion, ham and cheese and mix well. Cut the rolls into halves lengthwise. Place the bottom halves of the rolls cut side up in a baking pan. Spread the ham mixture over the top and replace the top of the rolls. Freeze, covered, at this point if desired. Sprinkle lightly with water. Bake, covered with foil, in a preheated 400-degree oven for 10 minutes or until heated through.

"Nothing Could Be Finer" Tailgating

Amber-Ritas

Box Car Bloody Marys

Not Really Turtle Soup

Smokey's Sausage Cups

Hallelujah Ham Loaves

Praline-Glazed Cheese

"Catch a Man" Dip

Buffalo Chicken Dip

Fresh Apple Cake

BAKED BRIE EN CROÛTE

SERVES 10 TO 12

1/4 cup packed brown sugar
1/4 cup pecans, chopped
2 tablespoons bourbon
1 sheet puff pastry, thawed
1 wheel Brie cheese
10 pear slices
10 green apple slices

Mix the brown sugar, pecans and bourbon in a bowl. Unfold the puff pastry on a lightly floured surface. Cut the rind from the cheese and discard. Cut the cheese horizontally into halves. Spread the pecan mixture over the cut side of the bottom cheese half. The pecan mixture will spill over the edge. Place the remaining cheese half cut side down over the pecan mixture. Place in the center of the puff pastry. Fold all four corners of the puff pastry carefully to the center of the cheese, pinching the seams to seal. Invert so the folded side is on the bottom and place on a greased baking sheet. Bake in a preheated 350-degree oven for 25 minutes or until light brown. Cool for 10 minutes. Serve with the pear and apple slices.

PRALINE-GLAZED CHEESE

SERVES 12

16 ounces cream cheese, softened
3 garlic cloves, minced
1 tablespoon grated onion
3 tablespoons butter
1/4 cup packed dark brown sugar
1 teaspoon Worcestershire sauce
1 teaspoon mustard
3/4 cup pecans, finely chopped

Mix the cream cheese, garlic and onion in a bowl with a fork. Shape into a disk and place on a serving plate. Chill, uncovered, for 15 minutes. Melt the butter with the brown sugar, Worcestershire sauce, mustard and pecans in a saucepan. Pour over the chilled cheese disk. Chill, covered, until set. Serve at room temperature with assorted crackers.

Buffalo Chicken Dip

SERVES 8 TO 10

8 ounces cream cheese, softened
12 ounces cooked chicken
1 cup hot red pepper sauce (for this recipe, Frank's® RedHot®
Original Cayenne Pepper Sauce was used for testing)
1 1/2 cups (6 ounces) shredded Mexican cheese blend

Spread the cream cheese in an even layer in a 9×9-inch baking dish or 9-inch pie plate. Shred the chicken into a bowl. Add the hot sauce and mix well. Spread over the cream cheese layer. Top with the Mexican cheese blend. Bake, covered with foil, in a preheated 350-degree oven for 20 to 25 minutes or until bubbly. Serve with pita chips, celery, carrots and/or tortilla chips.

"Catch A Man" Dip

SERVES 8 TO 10

2 cups (8 ounces) shredded sharp Cheddar cheese
2 cups (8 ounces) shredded mild Cheddar cheese
1 bunch green onions, chopped
1 1/2 (3-ounce) bottles real bacon bits
1 teaspoon cayenne pepper
1 1/2 cups mayonnaise, or to taste

Combine the sharp cheese, mild cheese, green onions, bacon bits, cayenne pepper and mayonnaise in a large bowl and mix well. Chill for 4 hours or longer. Spoon into a serving bowl. Serve with tortilla chips or corn chips.

SPICY SPINACH DIP

SERVES 6 TO 8

8 ounces cream cheese, softened
1 (10-ounce) can tomatoes with green chiles (for this recipe,
Ro-Tel was used for testing)
1 (10-ounce) package frozen spinach, thawed and well drained
2 cups (8 ounces) shredded Pepper Jack cheese
1 small onion, chopped
1 garlic clove, chopped
Salt and pepper to taste

Combine the cream cheese, tomatoes with green chiles, spinach, Pepper Jack cheese, onion, garlic, salt and pepper in a bowl and mix well. Spoon into a serving bowl. Serve with pita chips or crackers.

TOFFEE DIP

SERVES 8 TO 12

8 ounces cream cheese
1 (8-ounce) package milk chocolate toffee bits
(for this recipe, Heath brand was used for testing)
1/2 cup granulated sugar
1/2 cup packed light brown sugar

Place the cream cheese in a small microwave-safe bowl. Microwave on High for 1 minute. Remove from the microwave. Add the toffee bits and stir until the chocolate in the toffee bits melts, microwaving again if needed to melt the chocolate. Add the granulated sugar and brown sugar and mix well. Serve warm with apple and/or pear slices.

AMBER-RITAS

SERVES 10 TO 12

1 (12-ounce) can frozen limeade concentrate
12 ounces tequila
1 (12-ounce) can light beer (for this recipe, Bud Light was used for testing)
1/2 (2-liter) bottle diet lemon-lime soda (for this recipe,
Sprite Zero was used for testing)

Whisk the limeade concentrate, tequila, beer and soda together in a pitcher with a wine whisk. Serve on the rocks without salt.

Boxcar Bloody Marys With Cocktail Tomato Skewers

Serves 6 to 8

Cocktail Tomato Skewers
1 pint cherry tomatoes
1/2 cup vodka
3 tablespoons sea salt or celery salt

Bloody Marys
1 quart (4 cups) tomato juice (for this recipe,
Campbell's was used for testing)
1/2 cup beef broth
2/3 cup clamato juice
1 teaspoon horseradish
2 teaspoons Worcestershire sauce
1/2 teaspoon Old Bay Seasoning
Juice of 1 lime
2 teaspoons olive juice
1/4 teaspoon garlic salt
1 teaspoon hot pepper sauce (for this recipe,
Louisiana brand was used for testing)
1/2 teaspoon celery salt
1 1/2 cups vodka, or to taste
Pickled okra for garnish
Celery ribs for garnish
Green olives for garnish

To prepare the tomatoes, cut a small X at the end of each tomato. Cook in boiling water in a saucepan for 15 to 20 seconds. Remove with a slotted spoon and plunge immediately into ice water to stop the cooking process. Pop each tomato out of the skin from the scored end and place in a bowl. Add the vodka. Chill, covered, for 8 to 10 hours. Sprinkle with the sea salt. Thread onto skewers. Serve cold.

To prepare the Bloody Marys, combine the tomato juice, broth, Clamato, horseradish, Worcestershire sauce, Old Bay seasoning, lime juice, olive juice, garlic salt, hot sauce, celery salt and vodka in a pitcher and mix well. Pour into salt-rimmed highball glasses filled with ice. Garnish with the Cocktail Tomato Skewers, pickled okra, celery ribs and green olives.

POINT PARK PUNCH

SERVES 30

1 (8-ounce) jar maraschino cherries
1 (16-ounce) can pineapple chunks
2 cups lemon juice
2 1/2 cups sugar
3 (750-milliliters) bottles sweet Champagne
2 quarts (8 cups) sparkling water

Drain the cherries and pineapple, reserving the juice. Combine the reserved juices, lemon juice and sugar in a bowl and stir until the sugar is dissolved. Pour into a punch bowl. Add the Champagne, sparkling water, cherries and pineapple. Ladle into punch cups.

CAST-IRON COFFEE CAKE

SERVES 6 TO 8

3/4 cup (1 1/2 sticks) butter, softened
1 1/2 cups sugar
2 eggs
1 1/2 cups sifted all-purpose flour
2 teaspoons almond extract
Pinch of salt
1/2 cup sliced almonds
Sugar

Line a 9- to 11-inch skillet with heavy-duty foil, leaving the excess hanging over the side. Cream the butter and 1 1/2 cups sugar in a mixing bowl until light and fluffy. Beat in the eggs one at a time. Add the flour, almond extract and salt and mix well. Pour into the prepared skillet. Cover the top with the almonds. Sprinkle lightly with sugar to taste. Bake in a preheated 350-degree oven for 35 to 40 minutes or until the coffee cake tests done. Cool completely before serving.

Lodge Cast Iron is a family-owned business started by Joseph Lodge in 1896. Based in South Pittsburg, Tennessee, this company has been producing cast-iron cookware that is prized for its durability, heat retention, and distribution for more than 112 years. Nearly every classic Southern recipe, from fried chicken and corn bread to sauces and even cakes, can benefit from using cast-iron cookware in the preparation process!

BANANAS FOSTER FRENCH TOAST

SERVES *4 TO 6*

FRENCH TOAST
1/4 cup all-purpose flour
1 cup milk
Pinch of kosher salt
3 eggs
1/2 teaspoon cinnamon
1 teaspoon vanilla extract
1 tablespoon sugar
12 slices challah

BANANAS FOSTER SAUCE
1 cup firmly packed brown sugar
1/4 cup (1/2 stick) butter
1/3 cup water
1 tablespoon vanilla extract
3 ripe bananas, sliced

To prepare the French toast, place the flour in a large mixing bowl. Whisk in the milk gradually. Whisk in the kosher salt, eggs, cinnamon, vanilla and sugar until smooth. Heat a lightly oiled griddle or skillet over medium heat. Dip the bread slices in the batter until saturated. Cook on each side until golden brown. Keep warm in an oven until ready to serve.

To prepare the sauce, combine the brown sugar, butter, water and vanilla in a large saucepan and mix well. Cook over medium-high heat until the butter melts and the brown sugar dissolves, stirring constantly. Add the bananas. Cook for 1 to 2 minutes, stirring constantly. Pour over the warm French toast and serve immediately.

PUMPKIN STREUSEL MUFFINS

MAKES 1 DOZEN

STREUSEL TOPPING
1/3 cup crushed gingersnaps
1/2 cup pecans, chopped
1/4 cup confectioners' sugar
2 tablespoons butter, melted

MUFFINS
1 1/2 cups sugar
1/2 cup vegetable oil

2 eggs
1 cup canned pumpkin purée
1 2/3 cups all-purpose flour
1/4 teaspoon baking powder
1 teaspoon baking soda
1/2 teaspoon ground cloves
1/2 teaspoon cinnamon
1/2 teaspoon nutmeg

To prepare the topping, combine the gingersnaps, pecans, confectioners' sugar and butter in a small bowl and mix with a fork.

To prepare the muffins, combine the sugar, oil, eggs, pumpkin, flour, baking powder, baking soda, cloves, cinnamon and nutmeg in a large bowl and mix well with a spatula. Spoon into greased muffin cups, filling each three-quarters full. Bake in a preheated 350-degree oven for 12 minutes. Remove from the oven and sprinkle each muffin with the topping, pressing gently into each. Bake for 8 to 10 minutes or until the muffins test done. Loosen the muffins from the side of the cup with a small thin rubber spatula if needed and remove to a wire rack to cool.

TRICK-OR-TREAT BREAD

MAKES 2 LOAVES

1 cup vegetable oil
2 3/4 cups sugar
4 eggs
2/3 cup water
2 cups canned pumpkin purée
3 1/3 cups all-purpose flour
1/2 teaspoon baking powder

2 teaspoons baking soda
2 teaspoons salt
1 1/2 teaspoons vanilla extract
1 1/2 cups (9 ounces) semisweet
   chocolate chips
1 cup chopped pecans (optional)

Combine the oil and sugar in a mixing bowl and beat well. Beat in the eggs, water and pumpkin. Add the flour, baking powder, baking soda, salt and vanilla and mix well. Stir in the chocolate chips and pecans. Pour into two greased 5×9-inch loaf pans. Bake in a preheated 350-degree oven for 1 hour or until the loaves test done.

NOTE: Coat the chocolate chips with flour to keep them from sinking to the bottom of the loaves. Place about 1 tablespoon flour with the chocolate chips in a sealable plastic bag. Seal the bag and shake until the chocolate chips are coated.

SOUTHERN CORN BREAD

SERVES 6 TO 8

2 tablespoons corn oil
1 egg, lightly beaten
2 cups (heaping) self-rising white cornmeal
2 cups buttermilk

Pour the corn oil into a large cast-iron skillet and swirl to coat. Mix the egg, cornmeal and 1 1/2 cups of the buttermilk in a large bowl to form a batter slightly thicker than pancake batter. Continue to add the remaining buttermilk 1/4 cup at a time if needed to reach the desired consistency. Pour into the prepared skillet. Bake in a preheated 450-degree oven for 15 to 20 minutes or until golden brown. Broil during the last minute of baking for a deep golden brown crust, if desired.

The Mason-Dixon Line rarely comes up in our household, but it is firmly planted between our corn bread preferences. My husband was raised on the sweet, boxed variety, while I grew up viewing that recipe as an occasional oddity. Our family's reliance on corn bread is strong, and we need a workhorse recipe for the many uses in a Southern household: it must be firm enough to withstand the sopping of peas and greens, but absorbent enough for chicken and dressing; the crust must be crispy to provide a crunch among the various sauces and gravies it's served with, and it must be flavorful enough for an after-dinner dip in a glass of cold buttermilk. My husband now appreciates and enjoys Southern corn bread, and I compromise by making the sweet variety every now and then…but only for dessert!

Cut corn bread into 1-inch cubes and mix with chopped tomatoes, basil, olive oil, and vinegar. Add any chopped vegetables you prefer or hard-cooked eggs to create a Southern "panzanella," known as leftover salad in Italy.

Not Really Turtle Soup

Serves 10 to 12

1 cup olive oil
2 ribs celery, chopped
1 yellow onion, chopped
1/2 large green bell pepper, chopped
1/4 cup thinly sliced green onions
1 pound ground turkey
2 tablespoons paprika
2/3 cup all-purpose flour
6 cups very rich beef stock
1 large tomato, chopped
1/4 cup tomato purée
1/2 teaspoon cayenne pepper
1 teaspoon freshly ground black pepper
1 tablespoon kosher salt
1 tablespoon Worcestershire sauce
1 teaspoon thyme
1 tablespoon minced garlic
1 1/2 tablespoons fresh lemon juice
1/2 cup dry sherry
Dry sherry
2 hard-cooked eggs, minced for garnish
3 tablespoons chopped flat-leaf parsley for garnish

Heat the olive oil in a large stockpot over medium-high heat. Add the celery, onion, bell pepper, green onions and ground turkey. Cook until the vegetables are soft and the ground turkey begins to brown. Stir in a mixture of the paprika and flour. Add the stock. Cook until thickened, stirring constantly. Add the tomato, tomato purée, cayenne pepper, black pepper, kosher salt, Worcestershire sauce, thyme, garlic, lemon juice and sherry. Cook for 10 minutes or until heated through.

Place 1 teaspoon sherry in the bottom of each soup bowl. Ladle the soup into each bowl and garnish with hard-cooked eggs and parsley.

Note: This soup is named such because it's a turtle soup recipe made using ground turkey.

CURRIED PUMPKIN BISQUE

SERVES 6 TO 8

2 tablespoons butter or margarine
1 tablespoon onion powder
2 garlic cloves, minced
1 tablespoon curry powder
1 teaspoon ground cumin
4 cups chicken broth

1 (15-ounce) can pumpkin purée
1 cup sweetened or unsweetened
  applesauce
1 teaspoon sugar
Heavy cream to taste

Melt the butter in a large stockpot. Add the onion powder, garlic, curry powder and cumin and mix well. The mixture will be thick. Stir in the broth, pumpkin, applesauce and sugar. Bring to a boil. Reduce the heat and simmer for 20 minutes or to the desired consistency. Ladle into soup bowls and swirl in a splash of cream.

NOTE: The soup may be cooked for 20 minutes a day ahead and then warmed in a slow-cooker for 8 to 10 hours or to the desired consistency the next day. This recipe was awarded first prize at our "Brew and Stew" competition, part of our bi-annual Clean Sweep Fund-raiser.

Photograph for this recipe appears on page 118.

SPICY BUTTERNUT AND LENTIL SOUP

SERVES 6

1 large butternut squash, peeled and
  cut into 1/2-inch pieces
1 cup red lentils
5 cups water
2 tablespoons canola oil or olive oil
1 cup chopped onion
5 garlic cloves, minced
1 cup chopped celery

1 1/4 teaspoons salt
2 teaspoons curry powder
1/2 teaspoon coriander
1/4 teaspoon nutmeg
1/4 cup lemon juice
1 (15-ounce) can diced tomatoes
2 cups milk or plain yogurt

Bring the squash, lentils and water to a boil in a large stockpot. Reduce the heat and simmer, covered, for 30 minutes or until the squash is tender. For a creamy soup, purée and return to the stockpot at this point.

Heat the canola oil in a skillet over medium heat. Add the onion, garlic and celery. Sauté for 8 minutes or until the vegetables are tender. Add to the lentil mixture. Add the salt, curry powder, coriander, nutmeg, lemon juice and tomatoes. Return to a simmer. Stir in the milk. Simmer gently for 10 to 15 minutes. Ladle into soup bowls.

SWEET PECAN AND APPLE SALAD
SERVES 6

SWEET PECANS
1 egg white
1 tablespoon water
1 cup sugar
3/4 teaspoon salt
1/2 teaspoon cinnamon
1 1/2 to 2 cups pecan halves

CREAMY PECAN VINAIGRETTE
1/2 cup finely chopped pecans
1/4 cup maple syrup
1/3 cup apple cider vinegar
1/2 cup light mayonnaise
2 tablespoons light brown sugar
3/4 teaspoon salt
1/4 teaspoon pepper
1/2 cup canola oil

APPLE SALAD
9 to 12 cups chopped lettuce
1 Gala apple or a sweeter apple

To prepare the sweet pecans, whisk the egg white and water in a small mixing bowl until frothy. Mix the sugar, salt and cinnamon in a small bowl. Place one handful of the pecans in the beaten egg white and coat using a slotted spoon. Remove the pecans with the slotted spoon and place in the sugar mixture. Toss in the sugar mixture with another slotted spoon to coat. Spread the pecans in a single layer on a greased large rimmed baking sheet. Repeat with the remaining pecans. Bake in a preheated 250-degree oven on the top oven rack for 1 hour, stirring every 15 minutes to ensure even crispness.

To prepare the vinaigrette, combine the pecans, maple syrup, vinegar, mayonnaise, brown sugar, salt, pepper and canola oil in an airtight container. Cover the container and shake vigorously until mixed. Chill for 1 hour or longer before serving. Shake again before each use.

To prepare the salad, place 1 1/2 to 2 cups of the lettuce on each salad plate. Cut the apple into quarters and thinly slice each quarter. Top each salad plate with five or more slices of the apple and a small handful of the sweet pecans. Pour 3 to 4 tablespoons of the vinaigrette over each salad and serve. The vinaigrette is thick and will go a long way.

WEEKNIGHT SALAD

SERVES *10 TO 12*

2 heads romaine, torn into bite-size pieces
1 pint cherry tomatoes
3/4 cup pecan halves, toasted
1 cup (4 ounces) shredded Swiss cheese
1/2 cup (2 ounces) shredded Parmesan cheese
4 or 5 slices bacon, cooked and crumbled
2 or 3 garlic cloves, pressed
1/2 cup olive oil
1 teaspoon salt
Juice of 1 large lemon

Layer the lettuce, tomatoes, pecans, Swiss cheese, Parmesan cheese and bacon in a salad bowl. Store in the refrigerator for up to 24 hours before serving, if desired. Combine the garlic, olive oil, salt and lemon juice in a bowl and mix well. Pour over the salad just before serving and toss to coat.

PACIFIC RIM SALAD

SERVES *4*

2 tablespoons brown sugar
2 teaspoons soy sauce
2 teaspoons sesame oil
3 tablespoons rice wine vinegar
1 1/2 teaspoons red pepper flakes
1/4 cup vegetable oil
1 package mixed salad greens
4 green onions, sliced
2 (11-ounce) cans mandarin oranges, drained
8 ounces chopped cooked chicken
1/4 cup chow mein noodles

Combine the brown sugar, soy sauce, sesame oil, vinegar, red pepper flakes and vegetable oil in a glass jar with a lid. Seal the jar and shake well. Let stand for 30 minutes. Combine the salad greens, green onions, mandarin oranges, chicken and chow mein noodles in a salad bowl. Add the dressing and toss to coat.

Panini Tagliata

Serves 4

Dijon Sauce

1/2 cup sour cream
1/4 cup buttermilk
1 tablespoon Dijon mustard
1/4 teaspoon kosher salt
1/8 teaspoon freshly ground pepper

Sandwiches

4 cups arugula, trimmed
4 servings focaccia, split into halves horizontally
2 teaspoons balsamic vinegar
1 pound beef tenderloin, cut into 8 slices and pounded 1/4 inch thick
1/4 teaspoon kosher salt
1/8 teaspoon freshly ground pepper
1 teaspoon chopped fresh rosemary
1 tablespoon vegetable oil
4 large plum tomatoes, cut into halves lengthwise

To prepare the sauce, combine the sour cream, buttermilk, Dijon mustard, kosher salt and pepper in a bowl and mix until smooth.

To prepare the sandwiches, arrange the arugula over the bread bottoms and drizzle with the vinegar. Sprinkle the beef on both sides with the kosher salt, pepper and rosemary. Sear in batches in the hot oil in a skillet over high heat for 2 to 3 minutes or to the desired degree of doneness, turning once. Layer over the arugula. Place the tomatoes cut side down in the skillet. Cook for 5 minutes or until slightly charred, turning once. Place two tomato halves on top of the beef on each sandwich. Drizzle with the Dijon sauce and top with the remaining bread. Serve immediately.

NOTE: Leftover tenderloin from another recipe may be substituted in this dish. You may also substitute 4 hoagie rolls or 8 slices herb bread for the focaccia, if desired.

MOROCCAN BEEF

SERVES 4

1¹/4 pounds beef tenderloin, cut into 1-inch pieces
Salt and pepper to taste
2 tablespoons olive oil
6 ounces fresh baby spinach
2 garlic cloves, chopped
3 tablespoons sherry vinegar
1¹/4 cups apricot preserves
¹/2 cup drained mixed Mediterranean olives
4 cups cooked long grain rice
¹/4 cup chopped fresh flat-leaf parsley for garnish

Pat the beef with paper towels to dry. Season with salt and pepper. Heat the olive oil in a large sauté pan until hot. Sauté the beef in batches for 6 minutes or until evenly brown and medium-rare. Remove from the skillet to a plate, reserving the drippings in the skillet. Cover the beef to keep warm.

Place the spinach in a microwave-safe bowl. Microwave on High for 3 minutes or until wilted. Sauté the garlic in the reserved pan drippings for 1 minute. Add the sherry vinegar and continue to cook, stirring to scrape up any brown bits from the bottom of the pan. Stir in the apricot preserves. Bring to a simmer. Simmer for 2 minutes or until reduced to a sauce consistency. Stir in the olives, beef and spinach. Season with salt and pepper. Spoon over the hot rice on a serving platter. Garnish with the parsley.

Photograph for this recipe appears on page 118.

BOURBON ROAST

SERVES 6 TO 8

1 (2½-pound) eye-of-round roast, scored on each side
Garlic salt
Freshly ground black pepper
½ cup (1 stick) unsalted butter, melted
¼ cup Worcestershire sauce
¼ cup A.1. steak sauce
¾ cup bourbon
Juice from 1 lemon

Place the beef in a Dutch oven. Sprinkle with enough garlic salt until almost completely white on top. Sprinkle with enough pepper until almost completely black on top. Drizzle with the butter. Mix the Worcestershire sauce and steak sauce in a bowl. Pour over the beef. Pour the bourbon over the beef and then the lemon juice. Bring to a boil over high heat. Boil for 3 minutes or until the alcohol is burned off. Remove from the heat. Marinate, covered, in the refrigerator for 4 hours, basting occasionally.

Bring the beef to room temperature; drain, reserving the marinade. Place the beef on a grill rack. Grill over preheated medium coals for 20 to 30 minutes for rare or to the desired degree of doneness, basting with the reserved marinade.

MEAT LOAF FOR A KING

SERVES 6

2 eggs
¾ cup milk
½ cup panko (Japanese bread crumbs)
¼ cup finely chopped onion
2 tablespoons chopped fresh cilantro
1 teaspoon salt
⅛ teaspoon pepper
1 pound ground chuck
8 ounces ground pork sausage
¼ cup ketchup
2 tablespoons brown sugar
1 teaspoon dry mustard

Beat the eggs and milk in a bowl. Stir in the bread crumbs, onion, cilantro, salt and pepper. Add the ground chuck and sausage and mix well. Shape into a loaf and place in a shallow baking pan. Bake in a preheated 350-degree oven for 50 minutes. Spoon off the excess fat. Combine the ketchup, brown sugar and dry mustard in a bowl and mix well. Spread over the meat loaf. Bake for 10 minutes longer or until cooked through.

MELLOW MARINADE PORK AND RICE

SERVES 4

PORK

1 (1¹/2-pound) pork tenderloin (approximate weight)
Juice from 8 limes
¹/2 cup sesame oil
¹/2 cup soy sauce
Leaves from 1 bunch cilantro, chopped
8 to 10 green onions, chopped
Crushed red pepper to taste
¹/3 cup white wine

JASMINE RICE

Uncooked jasmine rice for 4
10 ounces fresh spinach
1 bunch fresh asparagus, trimmed and sliced
3 tablespoons sesame oil

To prepare the pork, tenderize the pork. Place in a baking dish. Add the lime juice, sesame oil and soy sauce, turning during each addition to cover the pork entirely. Add the cilantro and green onions. Sprinkle the pork with the red pepper, turning to coat. Bake in a preheated 325-degree oven to 155 degrees on a meat thermometer, turning after 15 minutes. Remove the pork to a cutting board and let rest for 10 minutes. Pour the pan drippings into a saucepan and add the wine. Cook until the sauce is reduced to a gravy consistency.

To prepare the rice, cook the rice in a large saucepan using the package directions for four servings. Remove from the heat. Add the spinach and asparagus. Cover and let stand until the spinach wilts. Add the sesame oil and mix well.

To serve, cut the pork into slices. Serve with the rice and gravy.

Mellow Mushroom opened its doors in February of 2002 and instantly became a local favorite. Located in the Coca-Cola Building in downtown Chattanooga, people are drawn to "mellow out" by the oversized Coca-Cola bottle cap awnings. Their signature spring water pizza dough and fresh ingredients are sure to satisfy any appetite.

YANKEE GLAZED CHICKEN

SERVES 4

1 1/2 cups apple cider
1/3 cup light corn syrup
2 tablespoons maple syrup or honey
1 tablespoon Dijon mustard
1 tablespoon white vinegar
1 1/2 teaspoons onion powder
1 1/2 teaspoons paprika
1 1/2 teaspoons garlic powder
1/8 teaspoon crushed red pepper
2 pinches of salt

2 pinches of ground black pepper
1/2 cup all-purpose flour
4 (12-ounce) chicken breasts, ribs
  removed and trimmed of excess fat
  and skin
2 teaspoons vegetable oil
1 large shallot, minced
  (about 3 tablespoons)
2 tablespoons apple cider

Whisk 1 1/2 cups apple cider, the corn syrup, maple syrup, Dijon mustard, vinegar, onion powder, paprika, garlic powder, red pepper, one pinch of the salt and one pinch of the black pepper together in a medium bowl.

Place the flour in a shallow dish. Sprinkle both sides of the chicken with the remaining salt and black pepper. Coat the chicken in the flour, patting off any excess.

Heat the oil in an ovenproof 12-inch skillet over medium heat until shimmering. Add the chicken skin side down. Cook for 8 to 14 minutes or until brown and sizzling, increasing the heat to medium-high if needed. Turn the chicken and cook for 5 minutes longer or until light brown. Place the chicken on a platter.

Drain the skillet, reserving 1 teaspoon of the drippings. Add the shallot. Cook for 1 to 2 minutes or until soft. Add the cider mixture and increase the heat to high. Simmer for 6 to 10 minutes or until thickened and reduced to 1 cup, stirring occasionally. Remove the skillet from the heat and tilt to one side so the glaze pools together. Use tongs to roll each chicken breast through the glaze to coat evenly and place skin-side down in the skillet. Bake in a preheated 375-degree oven for 25 to 30 minutes or to 160 degrees on a meat thermometer inserted in the thickest portion, turning the chicken halfway through baking. Remove to a platter and let rest for 5 minutes.

Return the glaze in the skillet to high heat. Cook for 1 minute or until the glaze is thick and syrupy. Remove from the heat. Whisk in 2 tablespoons apple cider. Spoon 1 teaspoon of the glaze over each chicken breast and serve with the remaining glaze on the side.

Given the geography and location between other large cities, it was inevitable that Chattanooga would become the location for many battles fought during the Civil War. With sites along Missionary Ridge, Lookout Mountain, Orchard Knob, and Chickamauga, visitors can spend a full day touring military parks and other attractions for history lessons that jump right off the page. It's the perfect outing for a picnic lunch!

HARVEST ENCHILADAS

SERVES 4 TO 6

1/2 whole roasted chicken
8 scallions, coarsely chopped
2 tomatoes, finely chopped, drained
and salted
2 teaspoons lime juice
1 (15-ounce) can pumpkin purée
5 garlic cloves
1 jalapeño chile, cut into quarters
and seeded

1 teaspoon chili powder
2 1/2 cups water
2 teaspoons kosher salt
1/4 teaspoon freshly ground pepper
8 flour tortillas (chipotle is preferred)
1 1/2 cups (6 ounces) shredded sharp
Cheddar cheese
Sour cream (optional)
Chili powder (optional)

Chop the chicken, discarding the skin and bones. Combine the chicken, scallions, one of the tomatoes and the lime juice in a bowl and mix well. Purée the pumpkin, garlic, jalapeño chile, 1 teaspoon chili powder, the water, kosher salt and pepper in a food processor. Pour 1 cup of the sauce in a shallow 2-quart baking dish. Spread the chicken mixture on one-half of each tortilla and roll up tightly. Place seam side down in a single layer in the sauce in the baking dish. Pour the remaining sauce over the top. Sprinkle with the cheese and remaining tomato. Bake in a preheated 425-degree oven for 30 to 40 minutes or until the sauce is bubbly. Remove from the oven and cool for several minutes. Serve with a dollop of sour cream and a dusting of chili powder to taste.

120

CHATTANOOGA CHICKEN AND PASTA

SERVES 6

1/4 cup (1/2 stick) butter
(do not substitute)
6 boneless skinless chicken breasts
1/2 teaspoon salt
1/2 teaspoon pepper
1 envelope Italian salad dressing mix

1 (10-ounce) can cream of
mushroom soup
6 ounces cream cheese
1/2 cup dry sherry or dry white wine
1 tablespoon chopped onion
Hot cooked pasta

Melt the butter in a slow cooker on Low. Place the chicken in the butter and turn to coat. Sprinkle with the salt, pepper and salad dressing mix. Cook, covered, on Low for 5 to 6 hours. Cook the soup, cream cheese, wine and onion in a small saucepan until creamy, stirring constantly. Pour over the chicken. Cook, covered, on Low for 30 minutes. Serve over pasta.

ROYAL BALLET TURKEY

SERVES A VARIABLE AMOUNT

1 turkey, neck and giblets removed
Salt and pepper to taste
1/2 cup (per pound of turkey) your favorite stuffing
(optional)
1 large onion, cut into quarters and layers separated
1/2 cup (1 stick) butter
1 cup white wine
1/4 cup soy sauce
1 tablespoon tarragon leaves
1 tablespoon chopped parsley
1 teaspoon pepper
1/2 teaspoon garlic powder
1/2 teaspoon onion powder
3 tablespoons lemon juice

Rub the turkey cavity with salt and pepper. Fill lightly with the stuffing and then truss. Place the turkey breast side up in a roasting pan. Place the onion around the turkey. Melt the butter in a saucepan. Add the wine, soy sauce, tarragon, parsley, pepper, garlic powder, onion powder and lemon juice. Cook over low heat until well combined. Pour over the turkey. Bake in a preheated 325-degree oven using the turkey package directions or to 160 degrees on a meat thermometer and golden brown, basting with the sauce at least once each hour and covering loosely with foil if the turkey begins to brown too quickly. Serve with the pan drippings or gravy.

SHRIMP CREOLE

SERVES 6

1/4 cup (1/2 stick) salted butter
1 cup chopped onion
1 cup chopped celery
1 small garlic clove, minced
2 tablespoons all-purpose flour
1 teaspoon salt, or to taste
1 teaspoon sugar
Dash of cayenne pepper
1 teaspoon paprika
1/2 small bay leaf
4 drops of Tabasco sauce, or more to taste
1/2 cup chopped green bell pepper
1 (19-ounce) can diced tomatoes
2 cups cooked peeled deveined shrimp
4 cups rice, cooked

Melt the butter in a skillet. Add the onion, celery and garlic and sauté until tender but not brown. Add the flour, salt, sugar, cayenne pepper, paprika, bay leaf and Tabasco sauce and mix well. Stir in the bell pepper and tomatoes. Cook over low heat for 10 minutes, stirring occasionally. Stir in the shrimp and cook until heated through. Discard the bay leaf. Spoon the shrimp mixture over the rice and serve.

Our hard work in the community has not gone unnoticed! In 2005 the Junior League of Chattanooga received the Corporate Philanthropy of the Year Award, given by the Southeast Tennessee Chapter of the Association of Fundraising Professionals. The award was presented at National Philanthropy Day, a celebration recognizing and honoring those who work tirelessly for others.

Easy-Peasey Skillet Mac And Cheesy

Serves 6

1 cup panko (Japanese bread crumbs)
Pinch of salt
1 1/2 tablespoons butter, melted
8 ounces elbow macaroni
1 teaspoon dry mustard
1 teaspoon water
2 eggs
1 (12-ounce) can evaporated milk
1 teaspoon salt
1/4 teaspoon pepper
1/4 cup (1/2 stick) unsalted butter
1 cup frozen peas
4 ounces cooked ham, cut into 1/4-inch pieces
3 cups (12 ounces) shredded Cheddar cheese, American cheese or
Monterey Jack cheese

Combine the bread crumbs, pinch of salt and 1 1/2 tablespoons butter in a bowl and mix well. Spread on a baking sheet. Bake in a preheated 350-degree oven for 15 to 20 minutes or until brown and crispy, shaking frequently.

Cook the macaroni in a large saucepan using the package directions; drain. Dissolve the dry mustard in 1 teaspoon water in a cup. Mix the eggs, 1 cup of the evaporated milk, 1 teaspoon salt, the pepper and the dry mustard mixture in a small bowl. Toss the hot macaroni with 1/4 cup butter in a large skillet. Add the egg mixture, peas, ham and 2 1/2 cups of the cheese. Cook over medium heat until the cheese begins to melt, stirring constantly. Stir in the remaining evaporated milk and cheese gradually. Cook for 4 to 6 minutes or until creamy, stirring constantly. Remove from the heat and let stand to thicken. Top with the toasted bread crumbs and serve immediately.

Photograph for this recipe appears on page 97.

123

A well-maintained skillet is not just a necessity to create a good Southern meal; it can also be an heirloom to pass down through generations. The key to cooking with cast iron is to keep it seasoned, preventing rust and creating a nonstick surface. To season a dry, clean skillet, brush lightly with vegetable oil inside and out. Place in a 400-degree oven upside-down on the top rack and bake for an hour. (Use aluminum foil on the rack underneath to catch any drippings.) Allow the skillet to cool in the oven before removing. Seasoning can be maintained by brushing the skillet lightly with oil after each gentle washing and drying.

GREEN BEANS BÉCHAMEL

SERVES 8 TO 10

2 pounds green beans, cooked and drained
1/4 cup (1/2 stick) butter
1/4 cup all-purpose flour
1 cup rich chicken stock
1 cup light cream
Salt to taste
Grated fresh nutmeg to taste
1/2 cup slivered almonds
1/2 cup (2 ounces) grated Parmesan cheese
1/2 cup cracker crumbs
1/4 cup (1/2 stick) butter, melted

Place the green beans in a buttered baking dish. Melt 1/4 cup butter in a saucepan. Stir in the flour. Simmer for 2 to 3 minutes, stirring constantly. Stir in the stock and cream. Cook until thickened, stirring constantly. Add salt and nutmeg. Pour over the green beans. Sprinkle with the almonds. Mix the cheese and cracker crumbs with 1/4 cup melted butter in a bowl. Sprinkle over the almonds. Broil in a preheated broiler until brown.

HARICOTS VERTS WITH
BLEU CHEESE AND PECANS

SERVES 6

1 pound haricots verts, trimmed
3 slices bacon
4 ounces crumbled bleu cheese
1 cup chopped pecans
Dash of pepper

Cook the green beans in a small amount of boiling water in a saucepan for 3 minutes or until tender-crisp; drain. Plunge immediately into ice water to stop the cooking process. Cut the bacon into 1/4-inch pieces. Fry the bacon in a skillet until crisp. Remove the bacon with a slotted spoon to paper towels to drain, reserving the drippings in the skillet. Add the green beans to the reserved bacon drippings. Cook over medium heat for 2 minutes. Add the cheese. Cook until the cheese melts. Stir in the bacon and pecans. Sprinkle with the pepper and serve.

BAKE'EM TWICE SWEET POTATO CASSEROLE

SERVES 10 TO 12

5 large sweet potatoes
1/3 cup butter, melted
3/4 cup granulated sugar
1/2 teaspoon kosher salt
2 eggs
1 teaspoon vanilla extract
2 teaspoons all-purpose flour
1 cup pecans, chopped
1/3 cup butter, melted
1/3 cup all-purpose flour
1 cup packed brown sugar

Scrub the sweet potatoes and wrap in foil. Bake in a preheated 350-degree oven for 1 hour. Let stand until cool. Maintain the oven temperature. Peel the sweet potatoes and place in a mixing bowl. Add 1/3 cup butter, the granulated sugar and kosher salt and beat until smooth. Beat in the eggs. Add the vanilla and 2 teaspoons flour and beat well. Pour into a greased 8×11-inch baking dish. Mix the pecans, 1/3 cup butter, 1/3 cup flour and the brown sugar in a bowl. Spread over the sweet potatoes. Bake for 35 minutes.

For more than seventy years, the League has supported Chattanooga's hospitals and medical services, particularly those that provide services to children. Our volunteers have operated baby clinics, day nurseries, training schools for nurses, and nutrition centers. The League was an original supporter of the Children's Hospital in 1929. Today we continue our commitment to improving our community with ongoing partnerships, outreach programs, and research to determine future health care needs in our area.

ROASTED VEGETABLE ORZO

SERVES 6 TO 8

1 small eggplant
1 large red bell pepper
1 large yellow bell pepper
2 small zucchini or squash
1 red onion
2 garlic cloves, minced
1/3 cup good-quality olive oil
Salt and pepper to taste
8 ounces whole wheat orzo
1/3 cup lemon juice
1/3 cup good-quality olive oil
2 1/2 teaspoons salt
1/2 teaspoon pepper
12 ounces feta cheese, crumbled
1/2 cup pine nuts

Cut the eggplant, bell peppers, zucchini and onion into bite-size pieces. Toss with the garlic, 1/3 cup olive oil and salt and pepper to taste on a large baking sheet. Roast in a preheated 425-degree oven for 40 minutes or until brown, turning once with a spatula.

Cook the orzo in boiling water in a saucepan for 7 to 9 minutes or until tender. Place in a large serving bowl. Add the roasted vegetables and pan drippings and toss to coat. Combine the lemon juice, 1/3 cup olive oil, 2 1/2 teaspoons salt and 1/2 teaspoon pepper in a small bowl and mix well. Pour over the orzo mixture and toss to mix. Cool to room temperature. Add the feta cheese and pine nuts and toss to mix. Adjust the seasonings to taste. Serve at room temperature.

"SAY GRACE" CORN BREAD DRESSING

SERVES 16

CORN BREAD

1 cup plain cornmeal
1 cup all-purpose flour
1 tablespoon baking powder
1/4 teaspoon baking soda
1 teaspoon (heaping) salt
3 tablespoons sugar
2 eggs
1/2 cup vegetable oil
1 1/3 cups buttermilk
Vegetable oil

DRESSING

3 or 4 ribs celery
2 onions
3 1/2 cups homemade or purchased broth
3 slices white bread
Milk
4 eggs, beaten
1/2 cup chopped onion
1/2 cup chopped celery

To prepare the corn bread, sift the cornmeal, flour, baking powder, baking soda, salt and sugar together. Beat the eggs lightly in a bowl. Add 1/2 cup oil and the buttermilk and mix until smooth. Add the cornmeal mixture and mix well. Pour 1/4 inch oil in a cast-iron skillet. Heat in a preheated 425-degree oven until hot. Add the batter. Bake for 25 to 35 minutes or until brown. Invert onto a plate and let stand to cool slightly.

To prepare the dressing, cut up three ribs celery and two onions and combine with the broth in a saucepan. Simmer until the vegetables are soft. Remove from the heat to cool slightly. Tear the bread into pieces in a bowl and add milk to cover. Drain the cooked celery and onions, reserving the broth. Drain the bread, reserving the milk. Crumble the corn bread coarsely into a large bowl. Add the drained white bread and the cooked celery and onion and toss to mix. Stir in enough of the reserved broth to make the consistency of oatmeal. Stir in the reserved milk. Adjust the seasonings to taste. Stir in the eggs. (The dressing may be made ahead and frozen up to this point. Thaw the night before baking.) Add 1/2 cup onion and 1/2 cup celery and mix well. Spoon into a large baking dish. Bake in a preheated 350-degree oven for 1 hour and 25 minutes or until firm and brown.

Aunt Issie passed this recipe down to her niece, a League member, from her famous restaurant in South Georgia called Daphne's Lodge.

DUCKIE'S BOOZY CRANBERRY SAUCE

SERVES 12

1/2 cup sliced apricots
1/4 cup sherry or orange juice
3/4 cup water
3/4 cup sugar
1/4 cup honey
2 tablespoons fresh ginger or crystallized ginger, finely chopped
1 (12-ounce) package fresh cranberries
2/3 cup chopped pecans (optional)

Soak the apricots in the sherry in a small bowl for 8 to 10 hours. Bring the water and sugar to a boil in a saucepan. Add the apricot mixture, honey, ginger and cranberries. Return to a boil. Cook over medium heat for 15 to 17 minutes or until reduced, stirring frequently. Remove from the heat to cool. Stir in the pecans.

NOTE: Plan ahead! Buy several packages of fresh cranberries around Thanksgiving and freeze for cranberry dishes later in the year.

CRANBERRY AND APPLE CRUMBLE

SERVES 10

4 cups chopped unpeeled Granny Smith apples
2 cups fresh cranberries
1 cup pecans, broken into pieces
1 cup granulated sugar
1/2 cup packed brown sugar
1 cup rolled oats
1/2 cup (1 stick) butter, melted

Layer the apples, cranberries and pecans in a 9×13-inch baking dish. Mix the granulated sugar, brown sugar and oats in a bowl. Spread over the layers. Pour the butter over the top. Bake in a preheated 350-degree oven for 30 to 45 minutes or until cooked through.

BREAD PUDDING WITH JACK DANIEL'S® SAUCE

SERVES *12* TO *16*

BREAD PUDDING

8 extra-large eggs

2 cups sugar

1 teaspoon salt

1 teaspoon vanilla extract

5$^{1}/_{2}$ cups milk

1 (16-ounce) loaf French bread, torn into pieces

$^{1}/_{4}$ cup pecans

$^{1}/_{2}$ cup (1 stick) butter, melted

JACK DANIEL'S® SAUCE

2 cups confectioners' sugar

1 cup (2 sticks) butter, melted

2 extra-large eggs, beaten

2$^{1}/_{2}$ tablespoons Jack Daniel's® Tennessee Whiskey

To prepare the bread pudding, whisk the eggs, sugar and salt lightly in a bowl. Whisk in the vanilla and milk until blended. Toss the bread pieces and pecans with the butter in a bowl to coat well. Spread evenly in a 9×13-inch baking pan. Pour the milk mixture over the top. Place the pan in a larger pan. Fill the larger pan with water to come halfway up the side of the smaller pan. Bake in a preheated 350-degree oven for 50 to 60 minutes or until a knife inserted in the center comes out clean.

To prepare the sauce, whisk the confectioners' sugar a small amount at a time into the melted butter in a bowl. Fold in the eggs, making sure the butter is not hot enough to cook the eggs. Stir in the whiskey. Serve warm over the bread pudding.

NOTE: If you are concerned about using raw eggs, use eggs pasteurized in their shells, which are sold at some specialty food stores, or use an equivalent amount of pasteurized egg substitute.

BERRIES 'N' CREAM

SERVES 4 TO 6

1 1/4 cups heavy cream
1 1/2 cups plain yogurt
3/4 cup packed brown sugar
3 cups blueberries or sliced strawberries

Whisk the cream and yogurt together in a large bowl. Sprinkle the brown sugar evenly over the top. Do not stir. Chill, wrapped tightly with plastic wrap, for 3 hours or longer.

To serve, remove the cream from the refrigerator and whisk to blend in the dissolved brown sugar. Place 1/2 cup of the berries in individual serving dishes. Ladle the cream mixture over the top. Garnish with the remaining berries and serve.

LUNCH COUNTER PECAN PIE

SERVES 8

1 refrigerator pie pastry
3 eggs, well beaten
1/2 cup sugar
3 tablespoons butter
1 cup light corn syrup (for this recipe,
Karo brand was used for testing)
1 teaspoon vanilla extract
Pinch of salt
1 cup pecans, chopped

Line a 9-inch pie plate with the pastry, trimming and fluting the edge. Bake in a preheated 350-degree oven on the middle oven rack for 7 minutes. Cool for 10 to 15 minutes. Combine the eggs, sugar, butter, corn syrup, vanilla and salt in a bowl and mix well. Stir in the pecans. Pour into the partially baked pie shell. Cover the outside edge of the pie with foil. Bake on the bottom oven rack for 50 to 55 minutes or until the pie is almost set in the middle. Do not overcook.

Store nuts and seeds in glass jars in the freezer to prolong shelf life and freshness. They can be used directly out of the freezer.

FRESH APPLE CAKE

SERVES 20

3 cups all-purpose flour
1 teaspoon baking soda
1 teaspoon salt
1 cup corn oil
2 cups sugar
2 eggs
1 teaspoon vanilla extract
3 cups ($1/2$-inch pieces) peeled Granny Smith apples
1 cup chopped pecans

Mix the flour, baking soda and salt together. Combine the corn oil, sugar, eggs and vanilla in a bowl and mix well. Add the flour mixture and mix until blended. Stir in the apples and pecans. The batter will be stiff. Spoon into a lightly greased 9×13-inch cake pan and spread evenly in the pan. Bake in a preheated 350-degree oven for 30 to 35 minutes or until a wooden pick inserted in the center comes out clean.

"TOOTIE'S" FUDGE CAKE

SERVES 9

$1/2$ cup (1 stick) butter, softened
2 cups sugar
1 cup all-purpose flour
1 tablespoon vanilla extract
$1/2$ cup baking cocoa
3 eggs

Combine the butter, sugar, flour, vanilla, baking cocoa and eggs in a bowl and mix well. Spoon into a greased 8×8-inch cake pan. Bake in a preheated 350-degree oven for 35 minutes. Serve plain or with ice cream or your favorite topping.

KIDS IN THE KITCHEN COOKIES

MAKES 1 DOZEN

1 cup granulated sugar
3/4 cup packed brown sugar
1/4 cup (1/2 stick) unsalted butter, softened
1 cup chunky or creamy peanut butter
1 egg
3/4 cup all-purpose flour
1/4 teaspoon baking soda
1/4 cup jelly

Combine the granulated sugar, brown sugar, butter, peanut butter and egg in a bowl and mix until smooth. Add the flour and baking soda and mix well. Roll into walnut-size balls. Place 2 inches apart on an ungreased cookie sheet. Make a small indention in the center of the balls with a spoon, being careful not to make the cookie too thin in the center. Place a small amount of jelly in each cookie. Bake in a preheated 350-degree oven for 8 to 10 minutes or until brown. Cool on the cookie sheet for 5 minutes. Remove to wire racks to cool completely.

132

As early as 1926, the Junior League of Chattanooga began fighting on the nutritional front lines by investing in the salary of the first nutritionist to teach in Hamilton County Schools. More recently, the League participated in the Association of Junior Leagues International's Kids in the Kitchen program, developed to address the rapid rise of obesity in America's children. Using fun, interactive lessons and demonstrations, the program teaches families how to prepare healthful meals and how to make exercising together fun!

Our president-elect's daughter, Sydney, invented these cookies one day in the kitchen with her mommy. Create your own back-to-school tradition by adding these to your child's lunch box!

TOUR TOFFEE COOKIES

MAKES 3 DOZEN

1 1/2 cups all-purpose flour
1 teaspoon baking soda
1 teaspoon salt
1/2 cup (1 stick) unsalted butter, softened
2/3 cup granulated sugar
3/4 cup packed light brown sugar
1 egg
1 egg white
1 teaspoon vanilla extract
1 1/2 cups old-fashioned oats
1 cup (6 ounces) semisweet or bittersweet chocolate chips
1 cup toffee pieces

Sift the flour, baking soda and salt together. Cream the butter, granulated sugar and brown sugar in a mixing bowl until light and fluffy. Add the egg and egg white and beat at high speed until combined. Mix in the vanilla. Add the flour mixture gradually, beating well after each addition. Add the oats, chocolate chips and toffee pieces and mix well. Drop by spoonfuls onto a greased cookie sheet. Bake in a preheated 350-degree oven for 10 minutes. Cool on a wire rack.

Since opening in 1930, millions of travelers have discovered Ruby Falls, located deep within historic Lookout Mountain. The 145-foot underground waterfall was stumbled upon in 1928 by cave enthusiast Leo Lambert during a nearby excavation. Today visitors travel almost a quarter mile by elevator, down through the rock, to explore caverns and admire this natural wonder. Ruby Falls, named after Lambert's wife, Ruby, is one of the deepest commercial caverns in the world and the most-visited underground waterfall.

A Season of Celebration

As the year draws to a close, we enjoy the bustle of activity while also reflecting on the meaning of the season. Festivities fill our days and nights, and we greet friends with good tidings. Stockings are hung, carols are sung, and the warm anticipation of what is to come helps blunt winter's chill.

The Grand Illumination lights up buildings all across town, spreading holiday cheer far and wide. Children excitedly visit Santa at the grand lobby of the Chattanooga Choo Choo, with Christmas lists in hand and wish on their tongues. Mothers and daughters take in sugarplum fairies and nutcrackers twirling across the stage at the historic Tivoli Theater, while atop Lookout Mountain visitors sip hot cocoa and stroll through the lighted gardens at Rock City.

Others choose to make new memories by creating a handblown glass ornament to give or hang on their own trees, or by taking a ride to pick out the perfect tree for trimming. We strive to share the spirit of the season with all those we meet, through both our actions and gifts. Winter is a season of celebrating traditions and tales, passed down across generations. Our homes form a comforting retreat as we spend time at the stove tending a soup pot and serve meals to loved ones that enrich us, in body and spirit.

Winter

Merry-Making on Christmas Eve

Coffee Punch

Creamy Peppermint Punch

Sun-dried Tomato and Pesto Torta

Beer Cheese

Dates en Brochette

Bûche de Noël

Eggnog Cake

Gingerbread with Molasses Sauce

Rudolph "in the Snow" Cookies

DATES EN BROCHETTE

SERVES 8 TO 10

1 (1-pound) package bacon
20 pitted dates
20 whole almonds

Cut the bacon slices into thirds. Stuff each date with one almond. Wrap a piece of bacon around each date and secure with a wooden pick. Store any unused bacon, tightly wrapped in plastic wrap, in the refrigerator. Place on a foil-lined baking sheet. Bake in a preheated 350-degree oven for 15 minutes or until the bacon is cooked through.

NOTE: *En brochette* means "served on a skewer." Pecan halves may be substituted for the almonds.

FIG AND GOAT CHEESE BRUSCHETTA

SERVES 20

1 1/4 cups chopped dried mission figs
1/3 cup sugar
1/3 cup coarsely chopped orange sections
1 teaspoon grated orange zest
1/3 cup fresh orange juice (about 1 orange)
1/2 teaspoon chopped fresh rosemary
1/4 teaspoon freshly ground pepper
40 (1/2-inch-thick) slices French baguette, toasted
1 1/4 cups crumbled goat cheese
5 teaspoons finely chopped walnuts

Bring the figs, sugar, orange, orange zest, orange juice, rosemary and pepper to a boil in a small saucepan. Cover and reduce the heat. Simmer for 10 minutes or until the figs are tender. Cook, uncovered, for 5 minutes longer or until thickened, stirring constantly. Remove from the heat. Cool to room temperature. Top each baguette slice with 1 1/2 teaspoons of the fig jam and 1 1/2 teaspoons of the goat cheese. Arrange on a baking sheet and sprinkle evenly with the walnuts. Broil under a preheated broiler for 2 minutes or until the walnuts begin to brown. Serve warm.

NOTE: The fig jam may be prepared up to 3 days in advance and stored in the refrigerator. Bring to room temperature before using.

BAKED MUSHROOM CAPS

SERVES 12

1 pound fresh mushrooms
1/4 cup crumbled cooked bacon
1 small onion, chopped
2/3 cup mayonnaise
1 1/2 cups (6 ounces) shredded Cheddar cheese
Pinch of salt
Pinch of pepper

Clean the mushrooms and discard the stems. Combine the bacon, onion, mayonnaise, cheese, salt and pepper in a bowl and mix well. Stuff into the mushroom caps. Place in a baking pan. Bake in a preheated 350-degree oven for 15 to 20 minutes or until the mushrooms are tender.

NOTE: The mushrooms may be prepared and stuffed 24 hours before baking. Refrigerate until ready to bake.

SUN-DRIED TOMATO AND PESTO TORTA

SERVES 12

1 (8-ounce) jar oil-pack sun-dried tomatoes, sliced
8 ounces cream cheese
1/4 cup (1 ounce) shredded Parmesan cheese
1 (7-ounce) bottle pesto (for this recipe,
Classico brand was used for testing)

Drain the sun-dried tomatoes. Do not rinse or pat dry. Cut the cream cheese into halves lengthwise. Arrange one-third of the sun-dried tomatoes in a rectangle the same size as the cream cheese halves or a bit smaller on a serving plate. Layer with one cream cheese half, one-half of the remaining sun-dried tomatoes and one-half of the Parmesan cheese. Cover with some of the pesto. Continue layering with the remaining cream cheese half, the remaining sun-dried tomatoes and the remaining Parmesan cheese. Cover with another layer of pesto, if desired. Serve with pita chips or baguette slices.

NOTE: You may prefer to pour the pesto over the top until it pools slightly around the bottom edge of the first layer. The torta may be prepared in advance and chilled for twenty-four hours before serving.

SMOKED SALMON SPREAD

SERVES 4 TO 6

1/3 cup finely chopped shallots
2 tablespoons unsalted butter
4 ounces smoked salmon, finely chopped
2 ounces (1/4 cup) reduced-fat cream cheese, or more as needed
3 tablespoons minced fresh chives
2 tablespoons minced fresh dill weed
2 tablespoons fresh lemon juice
Kosher salt and freshly ground pepper to taste

Cook the shallots in the butter in a small skillet over low heat until soft. Place in a bowl. Add the salmon, cream cheese, chives, dill weed and lemon juice and mix well. Add kosher salt and pepper. Shape into a ball or bar and place on a serving plate. Chill, covered, for 1 hour. Serve with assorted crackers and toasted bread slices.

NOTE: Use this spread to make **Smoked Salmon Ravioli**. Just place a tablespoon of spread between two wonton wrappers, seal with water and cook in boiling water for 2 minutes. Serve with melted butter and sour cream for a hot appetizer or light meal.

HOT BACON AND SWISS

SERVES 8 TO 10

8 ounces cream cheese, softened
1/2 cup mayonnaise
1 cup (4 ounces) shredded Swiss cheese
2 tablespoons chopped green onions
8 slices bacon, crisp-cooked and crumbled
1/2 cup crushed butter crackers (for this recipe,
Ritz brand was used for testing)

Combine the cream cheese, mayonnaise, Swiss cheese and green onions in a mixing bowl and mix well. Spoon into a lightly greased 1-quart baking dish. Top with the crumbled bacon and crackers. Bake in a preheated 350-degree oven for 15 to 20 minutes or until heated through. Serve with pita chips.

BEER CHEESE

SERVES 10 TO 12

16 ounces Cheddar cheese, shredded
8 ounces cream cheese, softened
1 garlic clove, chopped
1 teaspoon Worcestershire sauce

1 teaspoon Tabasco sauce
1/2 teaspoon dry mustard
1 cup (or more) beer
Red pepper to taste

Combine the Cheddar cheese, cream cheese, garlic, Worcestershire sauce, Tabasco sauce and dry mustard in a food processor. Add the beer gradually, processing constantly until smooth. Add red pepper and adjust the seasonings to taste. Spoon into a serving bowl. Chill, covered, until serving time. Serve with Melba toast.

PLANTATION EGGNOG

SERVES 12 TO 15

12 egg yolks
2 cups whiskey (for this recipe,
Jack Daniel's® Tennessee Whiskey was used for testing)
12 egg whites
2 cups sugar
1 quart (4 cups) heavy whipping cream, whipped
5 dashes of nutmeg

Beat the egg yolks in a mixing bowl for 20 minutes or until stiff. Beat in the whiskey. Beat the egg whites in a mixing bowl until frothy. Add the sugar gradually, beating constantly until stiff peaks form. Whisk the egg whites and whipped cream into the egg yolk mixture gently. Chill until serving time. Pour into 8-ounce serving cups and sprinkle with nutmeg.

NOTE: If you are concerned about using raw eggs, use eggs pasteurized in their shells, which are sold at some specialty food stores, or use an equivalent amount of pasteurized egg substitute.

Pardon me boys, is that the Chattanooga Choo Choo? Travel back to the golden age of luxury and visit the inspiration for the 1940s musical hit. Enjoy eating inside an elegant dining car at the Dinner in the Diner restaurant, sleep in a restored luxury railcar, and explore the grounds that served as the southern hub of railway travel for almost a century. Reopened in 1973 as a vacation complex, the Chattanooga Choo Choo and Terminal Station are now home to one of the world's largest model railroad exhibits. This Scenic City icon is a must-see for any visitor.

COFFEE PUNCH

SERVES 15 TO 20

1 cup sugar
16 cups hot strong coffee
1 gallon vanilla ice cream
1 cup whipping cream
1/2 cup chocolate syrup

Dissolve the sugar in the hot coffee in a pitcher. Let stand until cool. Pour into a punch bowl. Scoop the ice cream into the coffee. Stir in the whipping cream. Add most of the chocolate syrup and mix well. Drizzle the remaining chocolate syrup over the top for a pretty presentation. Ladle into punch cups.

Photograph for this recipe appears on page 137.

CREAMY PEPPERMINT PUNCH

SERVES 16

1 quart (4 cups) eggnog
1 (1-liter) bottle club soda, chilled
1/2 gallon peppermint ice cream
1 cup vodka
8 peppermint candies, crushed

Mix the eggnog, club soda, ice cream and vodka in a punch bowl. Sprinkle with the candies. Ladle into punch cups and serve immediately.

I Can't Believe It's Not Champagne!

Serves 16 to 20

1 (64-ounce) bottle white grape juice, chilled
1 (2-liter) bottle lemon-lime soda, chilled (for this recipe,
7-Up was used for testing)
2 tablespoons almond extract

Pour the grape juice into a large punch bowl or pitcher. Add the soda. Stir in the almond extract. Ladle into punch cups.

NOTE: To keep the punch cold longer, create a decorative ice ring using additional white grape juice and fruit such as grapes and star fruit slices. Freeze in a bowl or gelatin mold.

Photograph for this recipe appears on page 163.

Photograph for this recipe appears on page 163.

....

Warm Your Heart Wassail

Serves 10 to 12

1/2 cup water
1/2 cup firmly packed brown sugar
1/2 teaspoon cinnamon
1/4 teaspoon nutmeg
1/8 teaspoon ground cloves
4 cups cranberry juice
2 cups orange juice

Combine the water, brown sugar, cinnamon, nutmeg, cloves, cranberry juice and orange juice in a saucepan and mix well. Cook over medium heat until the sugar dissolves and the mixture is heated through. Pour into a teapot or coffee urn and serve.

PENCARROW HOUSE EGGS ON A CLOUD
SERVES 6 TO 8

EGGS
8 slices challah
8 egg whites, at room temperature
8 egg yolks

QUICK HOLLANDAISE SAUCE
1 cup (2 sticks) butter
3 egg yolks
Juice of 1 small lemon
1/8 teaspoon cayenne pepper
Kosher salt to taste

To prepare the eggs, place the bread on a baking sheet. Bake in a preheated 350-degree oven until the bread is lightly toasted. Beat the egg whites at high speed in a mixing bowl until stiff peaks form. Spoon the beaten egg whites several inches high onto each bread slice. Make a well in each egg white "cloud" and spoon an egg yolk into each indention, being careful not to break the yolk. Bake for 15 minutes or until the "clouds" are golden brown on top.

To prepare the sauce, place the butter in a microwave-safe bowl. Microwave on High until the butter melts and is very hot and foamy. Process the egg yolks in a food processor or blender for 1 to 2 minutes or until light and thick. Add the butter in a very slow stream, processing constantly. Add the lemon juice, cayenne pepper and kosher salt and mix well. Drizzle over the baked eggs and serve immediately.

NOTE: If you are concerned about using raw eggs, use eggs pasteurized in their shells, which are sold at some specialty food stores, or use an equivalent amount of pasteurized egg substitute.

> One medium lemon yields about three tablespoons of juice. Approximately five lemons are needed to make a cup.

ORANGE-GLAZED POPPY SEED BREAD

MAKES 2 LOAVES

BREAD
3 cups all-purpose flour
2 cups sugar
3 eggs
1 1/2 cups vegetable oil
1 1/2 cups milk
2 tablespoons poppy seeds
1 1/2 teaspoons salt
1 1/2 teaspoons baking powder
1 1/2 teaspoons almond extract
1 1/2 teaspoons butter flavoring
1 1/2 teaspoons vanilla extract

ORANGE GLAZE
1/2 cup sugar
1/4 cup orange juice
1/2 teaspoon almond extract
1/2 teaspoon butter flavoring
1/2 teaspoon vanilla extract

To prepare the bread, combine the flour, sugar, eggs, oil, milk, poppy seeds, salt, baking powder, almond extract, butter flavoring and vanilla in a mixing bowl. Beat for 2 minutes or until smooth. Pour into two well-greased 5×9-inch loaf pans. Bake in a preheated 350-degree oven for 1 hour or until the loaves test done.

To prepare the glaze, combine the sugar, orange juice, almond extract, butter flavoring and vanilla in a small microwave-safe dish and mix well. Microwave on High for 15 seconds or until warm.

Remove the bread from the oven and poke holes in the top with a wooden pick. Pour the glaze over the top slowly so the bread can absorb the glaze.

SAVORY WALNUT MUFFINS

MAKES 1 DOZEN

10 tablespoons butter, melted
2 eggs, lightly beaten
1 Vidalia onion, puréed
1 1/2 cups all-purpose flour
1 1/2 teaspoons baking powder
1 teaspoon salt
1 teaspoon pepper
3/4 cup (3 ounces) grated Parmesan cheese
1 1/2 cups walnuts, chopped

Whisk the butter and eggs in a bowl until blended. Add the onion. Stir in the flour, baking powder, salt, pepper, cheese and walnuts. Do not overwork the batter. Fill lightly buttered muffin cups two-thirds full. Bake in a preheated 375-degree oven for 35 to 45 minutes or until brown.

The Tennessee Riverwalk will ultimately form a twenty-mile greenway stretching along the Tennessee River from the Chickamauga Dam through downtown Chattanooga and out to Moccasin Bend. The Riverwalk's mission is to connect visitors to Chattanooga's parks, green spaces, museums, public art, shops, attractions, picnic areas, playgrounds, performance spaces, fishing piers, boat launches, and a rowing center via miles of scenic, restful walking trails and bridges. Through thoughtful, steady progress, this project demonstrates how Chattanooga has truly become a city reborn.

DADDY DOODAH'S MARRIED BEANS

SERVES 8

1 pound dried red kidney beans
1 pound smoked sausage, finely chopped
6 ounces pepperoni, finely chopped
1 (10-ounce) can tomatoes with green
    chiles (for this recipe, Ro-Tel
    was used for testing)
1 small can green chiles
1 yellow onion, chopped
2 garlic cloves, chopped
1 large ham bone with liberal amount of
    meat attached

1/4 teaspoon ground cumin
1/4 teaspoon cayenne pepper
2 bay leaves
1 bunch cilantro, large stems removed and
    leaves chopped
2 teaspoons sugar
Creole seasoning to taste
    (for this recipe, Tony Chachere's
    brand was used for testing)

Sort and rinse the beans in a colander under running water. Place the beans in a 6-quart stockpot and add 3 quarts (12 cups) water. Soak for 8 to 10 hours to soften. Cook the sausage and pepperoni in a nonstick skillet until lightly caramelized; drain. Drain the beans and return to the stockpot. Add 2 quarts (8 cups) water or enough to fully cover the beans. Add the sausage mixture, tomatoes with green chiles, green chiles, onion, garlic, ham bone, cumin, cayenne pepper, bay leaves and cilantro. Bring to a boil. Reduce the heat to low and simmer until the beans are soft, stirring occasionally to prevent the beans from sticking to the bottom. Stir in the sugar and Creole seasoning. Discard the bay leaves before serving.

NOTE: If the beans should accidentally stick, add an additional 1 tablespoon sugar and change stockpots.

This dish marries a Southern staple and a Southwestern favorite: southern Louisiana red beans and frijoles charro. The ham, sausage, and pepperoni should supply sufficient salt to the mixture. Taste the beans frequently, and if additional salt is required add additional Creole seasoning such as Tony Chachere's, keeping in mind this seasoning also has red pepper in it. If less piquancy is desired, just add salt to taste.

147

FESTIVE PEAR SALAD

SERVES 8

POPPY SEED DRESSING

$1/2$ cup sugar
$1/3$ cup apple cider vinegar
2 tablespoons lemon juice
2 tablespoons finely chopped onion
$1/2$ teaspoon salt
$2/3$ cup olive oil or vegetable oil
2 teaspoons poppy seeds

SALAD

10 cups torn romaine
1 cup (4 ounces) shredded Swiss cheese
1 apple, sliced
1 pear, sliced
$1/4$ cup dried cranberries
$1/2$ cup chopped cashews

To prepare the dressing, combine the sugar, vinegar, lemon juice, onion, salt, olive oil and poppy seeds in a bowl and mix well.

To prepare the salad, toss the lettuce, cheese, apple, pear, cranberries and cashews together in a salad bowl. Add the dressing and toss to coat.

MoonPies were born in 1917 from the ingenuity of Chattanooga Bakery salesman Earl Mitchell. They were created to satisfy the hunger of local coal miners, who were required to work long hours, often without lunch. They needed a snack with substance! Back at the bakery, Earl noticed workers dipping graham cookies into marshmallow and eating them after they had hardened. Inspired by this simple act, Earl added another cookie and covered the whole sandwich with chocolate. The new snack was a hit and now almost a million MoonPies are made and distributed daily.

WISH I WAS IN TAHITI AMBROSIA

SERVES 8

2 cups sour cream
1/4 cup sugar
11/2 to 2 (7-ounce) cans sweetened shredded coconut
2 (14-ounce) cans pineapple chunks, well drained
2 (10-ounce) packages frozen cherries, thawed and rinsed well
2 (14-ounce) cans mandarin oranges, well drained

Mix the sour cream and sugar in a bowl until the sugar dissolves. Stir in 1 can of the coconut. Add the pineapple and mix well. Fold in the cherries and mandarin oranges. Top with the remaining coconut. Chill, covered with plastic wrap, for 4 to 10 hours.

SLOPPY "EMMA VIRGINIAS"

SERVES 4 OR 5

1 tablespoon canola oil
1 onion, finely chopped
1/2 yellow bell pepper, finely chopped
1/2 orange bell pepper, finely chopped
2 garlic cloves, minced
11/2 ribs celery, finely chopped
Kosher salt and pepper to taste
1 pound ground beef
1 (15-ounce) can tomato sauce
1/4 cup ketchup
1 tablespoon Worcestershire sauce
4 or 5 hamburger buns, split

Heat the canola oil in a large skillet over medium heat. Add the onion, bell peppers, garlic and celery. Sprinkle with kosher salt and pepper. Cook until the vegetables are soft, stirring constantly. Add the ground beef. Cook until the ground beef is brown, stirring until crumbly. Stir in the tomato sauce, ketchup and Worcestershire sauce. Simmer until the mixture thickens, stirring occasionally. Sprinkle with kosher salt and pepper. Spoon onto the bottom halves of the buns and replace the top halves. Serve hot.

NOTE: As a twist on a traditional sloppy joe, this was served at a League member's daughter's birthday party in her honor. Insert your favorite person's name and make it a celebration dish in your home!

BEEF TENDERLOIN
WITH MARCHAND DE VIN

Serves 10 to 12

BEEF

1 (3-pound) beef tenderloin
2 tablespoons olive oil
1 teaspoon minced fresh garlic
1 teaspoon kosher salt
1/2 teaspoon freshly ground black pepper
1/2 teaspoon paprika
1/4 teaspoon cayenne pepper
1/2 teaspoon dried parsley
1/2 teaspoon dried basil
1/2 teaspoon dried marjoram

MARCHAND DE VIN

6 tablespoons butter
1/2 cup finely chopped onion
2 teaspoons minced fresh garlic
1/2 cup finely chopped scallions
1/2 cup finely chopped mushrooms
1/4 cup minced cooked ham
1/3 cup all-purpose flour
2 tablespoons Worcestershire sauce
2 1/2 cups very rich beef stock
1/2 cup dry red wine
1 1/2 teaspoons dried thyme leaves
1 large bay leaf
Kosher salt and freshly ground pepper
to taste

To prepare the beef, trim the fat and silver skin off the beef. Tie the beef with kitchen twine about 1 to 2 inches apart to make a uniform thickness, tucking under the slender end. Pat dry with paper towels. Mix the olive oil, garlic, kosher salt, black pepper, paprika, cayenne pepper, parsley, basil and marjoram in a small bowl to form a paste. Rub over the surface of the beef. Let stand at room temperature for 30 minutes. Place in a roasting pan. Place in a preheated 500-degree oven. Reduce the oven temperature to 450 degrees. Roast for 30 minutes. Remove from the oven. Wrap the beef in baking parchment and then in several layers of newspaper. Let stand for 30 minutes before carving.

To prepare the sauce, melt the butter in a saucepan over high heat. Add the onion, garlic and scallions. Cook until the vegetables are translucent. Reduce the heat to medium. Add the mushrooms and ham. Cook for 2 minutes, stirring constantly. Stir in the flour. Cook for 4 minutes, stirring constantly. Add the Worcestershire sauce, stock, wine, thyme and bay leaf. Simmer for 20 minutes or until thickened, stirring constantly. Season with kosher salt and pepper. Strain the sauce through a fine strainer or chinois, discarding the solids. Keep warm until serving time.

To serve, cut the beef into slices and place on a serving plate. Ladle the sauce over the beef.

NOTE: For parties or open houses, make the sauce the day before and reheat gently on the stovetop. Slice the tenderloin into single servings and serve with warm sauce in a chafing dish.

THE TERMINAL BREWHOUSE MAPLE MAIBOCK ROAST

SERVES 6

2 tablespoons vegetable oil
1 (3-pound) beef bottom round roast
1 large onion, julienned
1 tablespoon minced garlic
1 pint (2 cups) Terminal Brewhouse Maibock
1 tablespoon salt
2 tablespoons pepper
3 tablespoons finely chopped chipotle chiles with adobo sauce
1 quart (4 cups) rich beef stock
1/4 cup maple syrup
1/4 cup Dale's steak seasoning
3 tablespoons Worcestershire sauce
2 potatoes, coarsely chopped
2 carrots, coarsely chopped

Heat 1 tablespoon of the oil in a heavy roasting pan. Add the beef and sear on all sides. Remove to a plate and set aside. Add the remaining 1 tablespoon oil to the pan drippings. Add the onion and garlic and sauté until tender. Add the beer. Cook until heated through, stirring to scrape up the brown bits from the bottom of the pan.

Mix the salt, pepper, chipotle chiles, stock, maple syrup, steak seasoning and Worcestershire sauce in an ovenproof 8-quart stockpot. Stir in the beer mixture. Adjust the seasonings to taste. Add the beef. Wrap the stockpot loosely with foil and cover tightly with the lid. Bake in a preheated 275-degree oven for 2 hours. Add the potatoes and carrots. Bake, covered, for 1 1/2 hours. Remove the beef to a serving platter and let stand for 5 minutes before carving.

NOTE: For those outside the Chattanooga area, substitute your favorite Heller Boch beer for the Terminal Brewhouse Maibock.

In 1909 the Stong building was built and The Terminal Hotel was opened to complement the burgeoning Chattanooga Choo Choo. The Terminal Brewhouse revived the dilapidated space one hundred years later in January 2009 and now only world-class beer and fresh and exceptional foods make it to your table in eco-friendly ways.

Tex-Mex Stuffed Flank Steak

Serves 6

5 tablespoons canola oil or vegetable oil
Juice of 2 fresh limes
2 teaspoons kosher salt
2 teaspoons black pepper
1 1/2 teaspoons brown sugar
1 teaspoon ground cumin
1 teaspoon Mexican oregano
1/2 teaspoon thyme
1/2 teaspoon paprika
1/2 teaspoon red chile powder
2 1/2 pounds flank steak, trimmed and butterflied
3 fresh poblano chiles, or 4 Anaheim chiles
1 onion, thinly sliced
3 garlic cloves, minced
1/2 cup fresh cilantro, chopped
8 ounces tomatillos, thinly sliced
6 slices Monterey Jack cheese or Colby-Jack cheese
1 cup Heirloom Salsa Verde (page 19), or purchased salsa verde

Mix 2 tablespoons of the canola oil, the lime juice, kosher salt, black pepper, brown sugar, cumin, oregano, thyme, paprika and chile powder in a small bowl to form a paste. Rub on both sides of the steak and set aside.

Broil the chiles 4 inches from the heat source for 10 minutes or until roasted, turning frequently. Let stand until cool. Peel the chiles. Cut the chiles lengthwise to butterfly.

Heat 2 tablespoons of the remaining canola oil in a skillet. Add the onion. Cook for 5 to 8 minutes or just until beginning to soften. Add the garlic. Cook for 2 minutes or until tender and fragrant.

Lay the steak flat on a work surface with the long side facing you. Layer the cilantro evenly on the steak, leaving a 1-inch border. Layer a thin layer of the tomatillos, roasted chiles, onion mixture and cheese over the cilantro. Reserve any unused filling ingredients for another use. Roll up the steak carefully to enclose the filling and tie every 2 inches with kitchen twine.

Heat the remaining 1 tablespoon canola oil in a large ovenproof skillet. Add the steak roll-up and sear for 10 minutes or until brown on all sides, turning as needed. Bake in a preheated 350-degree oven to 140 to 150 degrees on a meat thermometer, or to the desired degree of doneness. Remove to a cutting board and tent with foil. Let stand for 20 minutes. Remove the twine and cut the steak into slices. Serve with a small amount of the Salsa Verde on top and pass the rest at the table.

NOTE: The steak roll-up can be prepared in advance, wrapped in plastic wrap, and stored for up to 1 day in the refrigerator before baking. Remove from the refrigerator 30 minutes before searing to bring to room temperature.

GRILLED TARRAGON LAMB

SERVES 8

1/4 cup olive oil
1 (8-pound) leg of lamb, boned, butterflied and trimmed
2 to 3 teaspoons freshly ground pepper
Salt to taste
3 tablespoons whole mustard seeds
3 tablespoons finely chopped fresh tarragon, or 1 1/2 teaspoons dried tarragon
1 1/2 tablespoons minced garlic
1/4 cup tarragon-flavored red wine vinegar
6 tablespoons butter

Place the olive oil in a baking dish large enough to hold the butterflied leg of lamb. Place the lamb in the dish and turn once to coat with the olive oil. Sprinkle each side evenly with the pepper, salt, mustard seeds, tarragon, garlic and vinegar. Marinate at room temperature for 2 hours.

Place the lamb on a grill rack, reserving the marinade in a large saucepan. Grill over preheated coals for 12 minutes on each side. Boil the reserved marinade for 3 minutes. Return the lamb to the saucepan with the hot marinade and dot with the butter. Let stand for 10 to 20 minutes before carving. Place the lamb on a serving platter. Pour the pan liquid over the top and cut into thin slices.

At the Tennessee Aquarium, experience the wonders of diverse freshwater and saltwater environments from cypress swamps and rainforests to tropical coves and undersea caverns. Housed in two glass-topped complexes on the banks of the Tennessee River, the Aquarium boasts thousands of living specimens. Visitors encounter giant catfish, ten-foot sharks, brilliant butterflies, red piranhas, macaroni penguins, frisky river otters, erratic alligators, and formidable jellyfish. Since its opening in 1992, the Tennessee Aquarium has been the centerpiece of the Chattanooga riverfront and a catalyst for downtown revitalization.

FRENCH QUARTER CHICKEN
SERVES 6

1 tablespoon olive oil
1 tablespoon butter
1/2 cup dry white wine
8 ounces mushrooms, sliced
1/4 cup chopped green onion tops
8 ounces cream cheese, softened
6 boneless skinless chicken breasts
2 tablespoons Dijon mustard
Dark brown sugar
Chopped walnuts

Heat the olive oil and butter in a large sauté pan over medium heat. Add the wine and mushrooms. Sauté for 5 to 7 minutes or until most of the liquid has evaporated. Add the green onions. Sauté for 1 to 2 minutes or until the green onions are softened. Remove from the heat. Cool for 10 minutes. Combine the cream cheese and mushroom mixture in a bowl and mix well.

Pound the chicken breasts 1/2 inch thick. Make an incision into the side of each chicken breast, making sure to not cut through the other side. Stuff 1 tablespoon of the cream cheese mixture into each incision. Roll up tightly and place seam side down in a 9×13-inch glass baking dish sprayed generously with nonstick cooking spray. Top each chicken breast with 1 teaspoon of the Dijon mustard and a generous sprinkling of brown sugar. Bake, covered with foil, in a preheated 375-degree oven for 30 minutes or until cooked through. Remove the foil and sprinkle the chicken breasts with chopped walnuts. Bake for 5 to 7 minutes or until the walnuts are toasted.

TABLE 2'S BLACKENED CHICKEN PIZZA

SERVES 12

6 large red bell peppers, cut into halves
Extra-virgin olive oil
Salt and pepper to taste
1 teaspoon salt
1/4 teaspoon cayenne pepper
1/4 cup extra-virgin olive oil
3 small boneless chicken breasts
Blackened seasoning to taste
2 tablespoons vegetable oil
1 large red onion, sliced and separated into rings

2 tablespoons Worcestershire sauce
Vegetable oil
1/4 teaspoon cayenne pepper
1 pizza dough shell from local bake shop
2 ounces provolone cheese, shredded
2 ounces mozzarella cheese, shredded
2 slices applewood-smoked bacon, cooked and chopped

Toss the bell peppers in a mixture of olive oil, salt and pepper to coat. Place on a baking sheet. Bake in a preheated 450-degree oven for 20 minutes. Maintain the oven temperature. Place the peppers in a bowl and cover with plastic wrap. Let stand for 15 minutes or until the skin loosens. Peel the bell peppers. Process the roasted bell peppers with 1 teaspoon salt, 1/4 teaspoon cayenne pepper and 1/4 cup olive oil until smooth.

Sprinkle the chicken with blackened seasoning. Heat 2 tablespoons vegetable oil in a cast-iron skillet. Add the chicken and sauté until golden brown. Remove from the skillet to cool. Cut into slices.

Toss the onion rings with the Worcestershire sauce, vegetable oil, salt to taste and 1/4 teaspoon cayenne pepper in a bowl to coat. Place in a baking pan. Roast until soft. (The onions may also be grilled or sautéed.)

Place the dough on a pizza stone or pizza tray. Ladle two-thirds of the bell pepper purée onto the dough and spread to the edge. Sprinkle with the provolone cheese and mozzarella cheese. Arrange the chicken, roasted onion and bacon on top. Bake according to the pizza dough directions until the cheese is bubbly and brown.

In 2007 Table 2 opened its doors in the Southside to present its passion to produce and deliver to its guests the highest quality and freshest meats and organic produce while supporting local farmers. The relaxed social atmosphere, in its chic refurbished location, is perfect for catching up with friends.

COMFORTING CHICKEN SPAGHETTI
SERVES *10* TO *12*

1 (3- to 4-pound) chicken, cut up
1 (32-ounce) carton chicken broth
3 cups whole grain thin spaghetti, broken into 3-inch pieces
1 (10-ounce) can cream of mushroom soup
1 (10-ounce) can cream of chicken soup
1 (10-ounce) can tomatoes with mild green chiles (for this recipe,
Ro-Tel was used for testing)
$^1/_2$ cup finely chopped onion
2 cups (8 ounces) shredded sharp Cheddar cheese
1 teaspoon seasoned salt
$^1/_8$ teaspoon cayenne pepper
Freshly ground black pepper to taste
1 cup (4 ounces) shredded sharp Cheddar cheese

Place the chicken and broth in a large stockpot. Add enough water to cover the chicken completely. Bring to a boil and boil for 5 minutes. Reduce the heat and simmer for 30 to 45 minutes or until the chicken is cooked through. Remove the chicken and set aside to cool. Reserve 1 cup of the stock. Return the remaining stock to a boil. Add the spaghetti. Cook until al dente. Do not overcook. Drain and set aside.

Shred the chicken, discarding the skin and bones. Mix the mushroom soup, chicken soup, tomatoes with green chiles, onion, 2 cups cheese, the seasoned salt, cayenne pepper and black pepper in a large bowl. Stir in the spaghetti. Add 2 cups of the chopped chicken and mix well, reserving any remaining chicken for another purpose. Add enough of the reserved stock to make of the desired consistency. Adjust the seasonings to taste. Spoon into a 9×13-inch baking dish. Top with 1 cup cheese. Bake in a preheated 350-degree oven for 45 minutes or until bubbly.

NOTE: This dish can be made in advance and frozen, or chilled for 2 days before baking. If time is short, use rotisserie chicken and cook the spaghetti in store-bought chicken stock.

SCENIC CITY SHRIMP AND GRITS

SERVES 4

GRITS

1 cup quick-cooking grits
1/4 cup (1/2 stick) unsalted butter
3/4 cup (3 ounces) extra-sharp white
    Cheddar cheese
1/2 cup (2 ounces) grated Parmesan cheese
1/2 teaspoon cayenne pepper
1 1/2 tablespoons paprika
1 tablespoon Tabasco sauce
Salt and black pepper to taste

SHRIMP

2 cups chopped smoked bacon
3 tablespoons extra-virgin olive oil
1 1/2 pounds (26- to 30-count)
    shrimp, peeled
Salt and pepper to taste
1 tablespoon minced garlic
3 cups sliced mushrooms
2 tablespoons lemon juice
3 tablespoons white wine
2 cups sliced green onions

To prepare the grits, cook the grits using the package directions. Whisk in the butter, Cheddar cheese, Parmesan cheese, cayenne pepper, paprika and Tabasco sauce. Season with salt and black pepper.

To prepare the shrimp, cook the bacon in a skillet over medium-high heat until the bacon begins to brown. Remove from the heat. Drain the bacon, reserving 2 tablespoons of the bacon drippings. Heat a large skillet until very hot. Combine the olive oil and reserved bacon drippings in the hot skillet. Heat until the oil mixture begins to smoke. Add the shrimp to the skillet. Season with salt and pepper. Sauté until the shrimp just begin to turn pink and the heat of the skillet increases. Stir in the garlic and bacon, watching carefully to prevent the garlic from burning. Add the mushrooms and quickly coat with the oil. Add the lemon juice and wine. Sauté for 30 seconds or until all of the ingredients are well coated. Add the green onions and sauté for 20 seconds. Serve over the hot grits.

Mise en place *is a French term that translates as "put in place." It means having everything ready to go before the cooking begins. It's a practice common in professional kitchens, and it's also a wonderful way to cook at home. Before starting any recipe, thoroughly read through the ingredients and instructions. Assemble all of the cooking tools you'll need to make the dish. Wash, prepare, and measure ingredients and have them within easy reach. You'll find that using this approach in your kitchen routine will cut down on cooking time and mistakes.*

158

NOT-A-CARBONARA PASTA

SERVES 4

1 tablespoon olive oil
1 tablespoon kosher salt
10 ounces angel hair pasta
4 slices bacon
1 tablespoon olive oil
1 1/2 cups Vidalia onions or other sweet onions, chopped
2 garlic cloves, minced
1 cup heavy cream
1/8 teaspoon red pepper flakes
1 cup frozen baby peas
1 cup water
Salt and freshly ground black pepper to taste
1/2 cup (2 ounces) freshly grated Parmesan cheese

Fill a large stockpot two-thirds full with water. Add 1 tablespoon olive oil and the kosher salt. Bring to a boil. Add the pasta and cook using the package directions; drain.

Heat a large nonstick skillet over medium heat. Add the bacon. Cook until crisp, turning frequently. Remove the bacon to paper towels to drain, reserving the drippings in the skillet. Add 1 tablespoon olive oil to the pan drippings. Add the onions and garlic. Cook over medium heat for 5 minutes or until the onions are translucent. Add the cream and red pepper flakes. Bring to a simmer. Simmer for 2 to 3 minutes.

Place the peas in a microwave-safe dish and add 1 cup water. Microwave on High for 30 to 45 seconds to defrost. Drain the peas. Crumble the bacon. Add the peas and crumbled bacon to the sauce. Simmer for 2 to 3 minutes or until the peas are tender and heated through. Season with salt and black pepper to taste. Remove from the heat. Add the pasta and toss to coat. Sprinkle with the Parmesan cheese.

NOTE: Because it does not contain eggs, this is not technically carbonara pasta, however it has similar flavors and inspiration.

COMPANY CARROT SOUFFLÉ
SERVES 6 TO 8

1 pound carrots, chopped
1/3 cup butter, melted
3/4 cup granulated sugar
2 tablespoons all-purpose flour
1/2 teaspoon baking powder
3/4 teaspoon vanilla extract
2 eggs, beaten
1 teaspoon confectioners' sugar

Cook the carrots in water in a saucepan until tender; drain. Mash the carrots. Add the butter, granulated sugar, flour, baking powder, vanilla and eggs and mix well. Spoon into a baking dish. Sprinkle with the confectioners' sugar. Bake in a preheated 325-degree oven for 30 minutes.

SPICY SOUTHERN GREENS
SERVES 4

2 pounds greens (collards, kale, mustard greens and/or turnip greens)
2 teaspoons salt
4 slices bacon, cut into 1/4-inch pieces
1 tablespoon unsalted butter
1 red onion, minced
3 garlic cloves, minced
1/2 teaspoon red pepper
1 tablespoon brown sugar
1 ham hock
1 cup (or more) low-sodium chicken stock
2 tablespoons cider vinegar
Pinch each of salt and black pepper, or to taste

Remove the stems from the greens. Rinse the greens well and chop. Bring water to a boil in a large stockpot. Add 2 teaspoons salt and the greens. Cook until wilted, stirring constantly. Cook, covered, for 8 minutes longer or until tender. Drain and plunge immediately into an ice bath or cold water to stop the cooking process. Let stand until cool. Squeeze as much water as possible from the greens and set aside.

Cook the bacon in a large skillet over medium heat for 8 minutes or until light brown. Remove the bacon to paper towels to drain, reserving the drippings in the skillet. Melt the butter in the reserved drippings. Add the onion. Sauté for 8 to 10 minutes or until the onion is soft and brown. Add the garlic, red pepper, brown sugar and ham hock and sauté for 30 seconds. Add the greens, bacon, stock and 1 tablespoon of the vinegar. Reduce the heat to medium-low. Cook for 15 to 20 minutes or until soft and tender. Stir in the remaining 1 tablespoon vinegar. Sprinkle with a pinch of salt and the black pepper.

MAMA'S MUSHROOM CASSEROLE

SERVES 8

1/4 cup (1/2 stick) butter
1 tablespoon Worcestershire sauce
24 ounces sliced mushrooms
2 garlic cloves, minced
1 1/2 cups herb stuffing mix
1 teaspoon salt
1 teaspoon pepper
2 cups (8 ounces) shredded Cheddar cheese
1/4 cup (1/2 stick) butter
1 cup half-and-half

Melt 1/4 cup butter in a medium skillet. Add the Worcestershire sauce, mushrooms and garlic. Cook until tender. Stir in the stuffing mix, salt and pepper. Layer the mushroom mixture and cheese one-half at a time in an 8×8-inch glass baking dish. Dot with 1/4 cup butter. Pour the half-and-half over the top. Bake in a preheated 325-degree oven for 30 to 40 minutes or until light brown.

NOTE: If using a metal baking dish, bake at 350 degrees.

ALMOND RICE

SERVES 4 TO 6

1/2 cup (1 stick) butter
4 ounces slivered almonds
2 cups uncooked rice
1 (10-ounce) can beef consommé
1 (10-ounce) can onion soup (not creamy)
1 soup can water

Melt the butter in a glass baking dish in a preheated 325-degree oven. Maintain the oven temperature. Sprinkle the almonds over the butter. Sprinkle the rice over the almonds. Pour the consommé and onion soup over the rice. Add the water. Bake, covered, for 1 hour. Stir in a small amount of hot water if the rice becomes too dry.

TUXEDO TRUFFLE COOKIES

MAKES 2 1/2 DOZEN

1/4 cup (1/2 stick) unsalted butter, cut into cubes
1/2 cup (3 ounces) semisweet chocolate chips
1 egg
1/3 cup granulated sugar
1/3 cup packed brown sugar
1/2 teaspoon vanilla extract
1/8 teaspoon peppermint extract
1 cup all-purpose flour
1/3 cup baking cocoa
1/4 teaspoon baking powder
1/8 teaspoon salt
1 3/4 cups mint chocolate chips (for this recipe,
Andes Crème de Menthe Baking Chips were used for testing)
1 cup (6 ounces) semisweet chocolate chips
2 tablespoons butter
1 1/2 cups white or vanilla chips

Melt 1/4 cup butter and 1/2 cup semisweet chocolate chips in a small saucepan over low heat. Remove from the heat and stir until smooth. Cool slightly. Place in a medium bowl. Stir in the egg, granulated sugar, brown sugar, vanilla and peppermint extract and mix well. Mix the flour, baking cocoa, baking powder and salt together. Stir into the chocolate mixture. Fold in 3/4 cup of the mint chocolate chips. Shape rounded tablespoonfuls of the dough into balls. Place 2 inches apart on ungreased cookie sheets. Bake in a preheated 350-degree oven for 8 to 10 minutes or until the tops appear slightly dry. Cool on the cookie sheet for 1 minute. Remove to wire racks to cool completely.

Combine 1 tablespoon of the butter, the remaining 1 cup mint chocolate chips and 1 cup semisweet chocolate chips in a microwave-safe bowl. Microwave on High at 30-second intervals until soft. Stir until smooth. Dip one-half of the cookies halfway into the chocolate mixture. Cool on baking parchment until set.

Combine the remaining 1 tablespoon butter and the white chips in a microwave-safe bowl. Microwave on High at 30-second intervals until soft. Stir until smooth. Dip the remaining cookies halfway in the vanilla mixture. Cool on baking parchment until set.

Photograph for this recipe appears at right.

Cocktails and Cheer

I Can't Believe It's Not Champagne!
Hot and Bacon Swiss
Festive Pear Salad
Beef Tenderloin with Marchand de Vin
Smoked Salmon Ravioli
Company Carrot Soufflé
Winter White Chocolate Macaroons
Tuxedo Truffle Cookies
Warm Your Heart Wassail

Winter White Chocolate Macaroons

Makes 3 Dozen

2²/3 cups flaked coconut
3 ounces white chocolate, finely chopped
²/3 cup sugar
1/4 cup plus 2 tablespoons all-purpose flour
1/4 teaspoon salt
2 egg whites
1 teaspoon almond extract

Mix the coconut, white chocolate, sugar, flour and salt in a large bowl. Stir in the egg whites and almond extract. Drop by tablespoonfuls onto a greased cookie sheet. Bake in a preheated 325-degree oven for 17 to 20 minutes or until the edges are golden brown. Remove immediately from the cookie sheet to a wire rack to cool.

Lemon Snowflakes

Makes 5 to 6 Dozen

1 (2-layer) package lemon cake mix
1 (4-ounce) package lemon instant pudding mix
1 egg
2¹/4 cups whipped topping
2 cups confectioners' sugar

Beat the cake mix, pudding mix, egg and whipped topping at medium speed in a mixing bowl until blended. The batter will be very sticky. Drop by teaspoonfuls into confectioners' sugar and roll lightly to coat. Place on ungreased baking sheets. Bake in a preheated 350-degree oven for 10 to 12 minutes or until light brown. Cool on a wire rack.

Photograph for this recipe appears on page 153.

Rudolph "In The Snow" Cookies

Makes 2 dozen

2 cups all-purpose flour
$1/2$ tablespoon baking powder
$3/4$ teaspoon baking soda
$1/2$ teaspoon salt
1 cup (2 sticks) butter, softened
1 cup packed light brown sugar
1 egg
2 teaspoons vanilla extract
$1^1/2$ cups chopped macadamia nuts
$3/4$ cup white chocolate chips
2 cups dried cranberries (for this recipe,
Craisins were used for testing)

Mix the flour, baking powder, baking soda and salt together. Beat the butter in a mixing bowl for 2 minutes or until fluffy. Add the brown sugar and mix well. Beat in the egg and vanilla. Add the flour one-third at a time, beating well after each addition. Stir in the macadamia nuts, white chocolate chips and dried cranberries. Roll into small round balls and place on a cookie sheet. Bake in a preheated 350-degree oven for 8 to 10 minutes or until golden brown.

Flying reindeer enjoy sweets too! Make Magic Reindeer Food by mixing $1/4$ cup rolled oats with 1 tablespoon candy sugar and sprinkle on the lawn when setting out those cookies for Santa!

Photograph for this recipe appears on page 137.

165

Chocolate Gravy

Serves 4

$1^3/4$ cups sugar
$3/4$ cup baking cocoa
$1/2$ cup all-purpose flour
3 cups water
2 tablespoons butter

Mix the sugar, baking cocoa and flour in a large saucepan or cast-iron skillet. Add the water. Bring to a rolling boil. Add the butter and reduce the heat to medium. Cook for 3 minutes or until the consistency of gravy, stirring constantly. Remove from the heat and serve.

NOTE: This can be served atop biscuits for a delicious dessert and is also good over peppermint ice cream for a festive treat.

ANGEL FOOD PIE

SERVES 6 TO 8

4¹/2 tablespoons cornstarch
³/4 cup granulated sugar
1¹/2 cups boiling water
3 egg whites, at room temperature
3 tablespoons granulated sugar
Pinch of salt
1 teaspoon vanilla extract
1 baked (10-inch) pie shell
1 cup heavy whipping cream
Confectioners' sugar
1 milk chocolate candy bar, frozen and grated

Cook the cornstarch, ³/4 cup granulated sugar and boiling water in a double boiler until thick and clear, stirring constantly. Beat the egg whites in a mixing bowl until stiff peaks form. Add 3 tablespoons granulated sugar, the salt and vanilla. Add the hot sugar mixture gradually, beating constantly until creamy. Let stand until cool. Spoon into the baked pie shell. Chill in the refrigerator. Beat the whipping cream and confectioners' sugar to taste in a mixing bowl until firm. Spread over the top of the pie. Sprinkle with the chocolate.

NOTE: If you are concerned about using raw egg whites, use eggs pasteurized in their shells, which are sold at some specialty food stores, or use an equivalent amount of pasteurized egg white substitute.

Photograph for this recipe appears on page 153.

A League member learned to make this pie for her husband in order to carry on the tradition his mother started. This has been his annual birthday pie for over sixty years!

Bûche De Noël

Serves 6 to 8

Meringue Mushrooms
4 egg whites, at room temperature
1/2 teaspoon cream of tartar
1 cup sugar
1 tablespoon baking cocoa
2 ounces milk chocolate squares or chips

Chocolate Filling
1 (4-ounce) package chocolate instant pudding mix
2 teaspoons baking cocoa

1/2 cup milk
Dash of salt
2 cups whipped topping

Cake
1 package angel food cake mix
1 1/2 tablespoons baking cocoa
Confectioners' sugar
2 (16-ounce) cans milk chocolate frosting
1/4 cup confectioners' sugar

To prepare the meringue mushrooms, line two baking sheets with foil or baking parchment. Beat the egg whites and cream of tartar at high speed in a mixing bowl until soft peaks form. Add the sugar gradually, beating until stiff peaks form. Spoon into a large pastry bag fitted with a 1/2-inch tip or into a sealable plastic bag with the corner cut off. Pipe into wide, round mounds about 1 1/2 inches in diameter (to resemble mushroom caps) on the prepared baking sheets. Smooth the tops. Sift the baking cocoa over the tops. Pipe the remaining meringue into thin 1-inch tall towers to resemble mushroom stems. Bake in a preheated 200-degree oven for 2 hours or until the meringues are crisp and dry. Turn off the oven and let cool completely in the oven. Melt the chocolate in a small saucepan over low heat. Spread the underside of the mushroom caps with the melted chocolate and attach the stems. Trim the tops of the stems with scissors for a more even attachment, if needed. Place the mushrooms upside down on a tray. Let stand for 1 hour or until the chocolate sets.

To prepare the filling, combine the pudding mix, baking cocoa, milk and salt in a bowl and mix until smooth and thick. Fold in the whipped topping.

To prepare the cake, line a 12×18-inch jelly roll pan with baking parchment or waxed paper. Prepare the cake mix using the package directions, adding the baking cocoa. Pour into the prepared pan. Bake in a preheated 350-degree oven for 15 minutes or until set. Spread two or three clean lint-free flour sack towels on a work surface and dust with confectioners' sugar. Remove the cake from the oven and invert onto the prepared towels, using a butter knife to slowly remove the cake from the pan. Remove the baking parchment and discard. Roll the warm cake in the towel from the short side and place on a wire rack to cool. Unroll the cooled cake carefully and remove the towel. Spread the filling to within 1 inch of the edge and reroll. Place seam side down on a serving plate. Spread the frosting over the cake, using an offset spatula to run back and forth against the frosting to resemble the texture of tree bark. Place the meringue mushrooms all along the side and top of the cake. Sprinkle with 1/4 cup confectioners' sugar for a snowy effect.

NOTE: For extra pizzazz in presentation, before frosting, slice off about 2 to 3 inches of the end of the log and place on top of, or on the side of the cake to resemble a cut-off branch. The meringue mushrooms can be made several days in advance and stored in airtight containers until ready to use.

EGGNOG CAKE

SERVES *16*

1 package angel food cake mix
1 tablespoon unflavored gelatin
1/2 cup milk
3 egg yolks
1/4 cup bourbon
1/2 cup sugar
1 cup heavy whipping cream, whipped
3 egg whites, stiffly beaten
1 cup heavy whipping cream
2 tablespoons sugar
1 teaspoon vanilla extract
Candied fruit, pecans or nutmeg for garnish

Prepare the cake mix and bake using the package directions. Cool the cake and remove from the pan. Cut out the center of the cake, increasing the hole by 2 inches. Soften the gelatin in the milk in a double boiler. Heat over hot water until the gelatin dissolves. Beat the egg yolks in a mixing bowl until thick. Add the gelatin mixture gradually, beating constantly. Beat in the bourbon and 1/2 cup sugar. Fold in the whipped cream. Fold in the egg whites. Chill until the mixture begins to set. Fill the cake cavity, spreading any remaining mousse over the top of the cake.

Beat the whipping cream, 2 tablespoons sugar and vanilla in a mixing bowl until firm. Spread the whipped cream over the top and side of the cake. Garnish with candied fruit, pecans or nutmeg.

NOTE: If you are concerned about using raw eggs, use eggs pasteurized in their shells, which are sold at some specialty food stores, or use an equivalent amount of pasteurized egg substitute.

NONIE'S CHOCOLATE CAKE

SERVES 20 TO 25

CAKE

2$^{1}/_{2}$ cups sifted cake flour

1 teaspoon baking soda

$^{1}/_{2}$ teaspoon salt

1 (4-ounce) bar German's sweet chocolate

$^{1}/_{2}$ cup boiling water

1 cup (2 sticks) butter, softened

2 cups sugar

4 egg yolks

1 teaspoon vanilla extract

1 cup buttermilk

4 egg whites, stiffly beaten

CHOCOLATE COFFEE FROSTING

$^{1}/_{2}$ cup (1 stick) butter

5 ounces semisweet chocolate

1 teaspoon (heaping) instant coffee granules

1 cup boiling water

1 teaspoon vanilla extract

1 (1-pound) package confectioners' sugar

To prepare the cake, line two 9-inch cake pans with waxed paper. Butter the waxed paper. Sift the cake flour, baking soda and salt together. Melt the chocolate in the water in a bowl. Let stand until cool. Cream the butter and sugar in a mixing bowl until light. Add the egg yolks and beat well. Add the vanilla and melted chocolate. Add the flour mixture alternately with the buttermilk, beating well after each addition and ending with the buttermilk. Fold in the egg whites. Pour into the prepared cake pans. Bake in a preheated 350-degree oven for 30 to 35 minutes or until wooden picks inserted in the layers come out clean. Cool in the pans for 10 minutes. Invert onto cake racks to cool completely. Remove the waxed paper.

To prepare the frosting, melt the butter in a small saucepan. Add the chocolate and stir until smooth. Dissolve the coffee granules in the boiling water. Stir the chocolate mixture and vanilla together in a mixing bowl. Add the confectioners' sugar and 7 tablespoons of the hot coffee alternately, beating well after each addition. Reserve the remaining coffee for another purpose.

To assemble, place one cake layer flat side up on a cake plate. Spread the frosting over the top. Place the remaining cake layer flat side down on top of the first layer. Frost the top and side of the cake.

To prevent cake from sticking to the cake pan, cut a piece of waxed paper the size and shape of the pan and insert in the bottom of the pan before adding the batter.

MOTHER'S FRUITCAKE
MAKES 2 LOAVES

FRUITCAKE
1 teaspoon baking soda
1/2 cup buttermilk
3 1/2 cups all-purpose flour
1 pound chopped dates
1 pound raisins
1 pound chopped candy orange slices
1 pound chopped pineapple
1 pound chopped cherries
2 cups chopped pecans
1 (3-ounce) can flaked coconut
1 cup (2 sticks) butter, softened
2 cups sugar
4 eggs

ORANGE GLAZE
1 cup orange juice
2 cups confectioners' sugar

To prepare the fruitcake, dissolve the baking soda in the buttermilk in a small bowl. Mix the flour, dates, raisins, orange slices, pineapple, cherries and pecans in a large bowl to coat. Stir in the coconut. Cream the butter and sugar in a mixing bowl until light and fluffy. Add the eggs one at a time, beating well after each addition. Mix in the buttermilk mixture. Add the fruit mixture and mix well by hand. The dough will be very stiff. Fill two large greased 5×8-inch loaf pans nearly full. Bake in a preheated 250-degree oven for 2 1/2 to 3 hours. The batter will not rise much.

To prepare the glaze, beat the orange juice and confectioners' sugar in a bowl until smooth. Pour over the hot cake. Let stand in the pan for 8 to 10 hours before serving.

Photograph for this recipe appears on page 153.

GINGERBREAD WITH MOLASSES SAUCE

SERVES 8 TO 10

GINGERBREAD

2 cups all-purpose flour
1 teaspoon baking soda
4 to 6 tablespoons butter
2 tablespoons molasses (for this recipe,
Alaga brand was used for testing)
1 cup sugar
1 teaspoon salt
1 teaspoon cinnamon
1/2 teaspoon ground cloves
1/4 teaspoon ground ginger
1 egg
1 cup buttermilk

MOLASSES SAUCE

1 cup sugar
1 cup milk
1/2 cup (1 stick) butter
1 cup cane syrup (for this recipe, Alaga brand was used for testing)
1 teaspoon ginger

To prepare the gingerbread, sift the flour and baking soda together. Place the butter in a microwave-safe bowl. Microwave on High until melted. Add the molasses and sugar. Stir in the salt, cinnamon, cloves and ginger and mix well. Beat in the egg. Add the flour mixture alternately with the buttermilk, mixing well after each addition. Spoon into a greased and floured 8×8-inch or 9×9-inch baking pan. Bake in a preheated 400-degree oven for 30 to 35 minutes or until the bread tests done.

To prepare the sauce, bring the sugar, milk, butter, cane syrup and ginger to a boil in a saucepan. Cook until the sauce thickens, stirring constantly. Serve warm or at room temperature with the warm gingerbread.

Cookbook Committee

CORE COMMITTEE

Chair: Billie Rose
Assistant Chair: Rebecca Brinkley
Assistant Chair: Theresa Critchfield
Art & Design Chair: Christy Fazio Clegg
Recipe Chair: Ginger Birnbaum
Non-Recipe Text Chair: Jill Glenn
Marketing Chair: Lindsay Wolford
Assistant Marketing Chair: Jasmin Rippon

COMMITTEE MEMBERS

Art & Design Committee
Elizabeth Campbell
Rhymes Stabler

Recipe Committee
Anna Adamson
Taylor Andersen
Molly Beard
Laura Jennings
Emmie Treadwell

Non-Recipe Text Committee
Kimber Bastone
Kristin Leach
Brooke Maedel

Marketing Committee
Angela Ballard
Cristy DeBaby-Blanding
Ashley Manning
Beth McKenzie
Chrissy Nolan
Karen Underwood

Sustainer Liaison
Ellen Epperson

Tour Du Jour Liaison
Heather Sveadas

Executive Board
2009–2010

President: Missy McKenna

President-Elect: Missy Elliott

Communications Vice President: Shelley McGraw

Finance Vice President: Jennifer Franklin

Membership Vice President: Kathryn Campbell

Programs Vice President: Kelly Reese

Treasurer: Cynthia Fagan

Executive Coordinator: Rebecca Brinkley

Recording Secretary: Amanda Kelley

Nominating & Placement: Ashley Farless

Executive Board
2010–2011

President: Missy Elliott

President-Elect: Jennifer Franklin

Communications Vice President: Scottie Goodman Summerlin

Finance Vice President: Cynthia Fagan

Membership Vice President: Karen Leavengood

Programs Vice President: Leigh Todd

Treasurer: Kelly Reese

Executive Coordinator: Rebecca Davenport

Recording Secretary: Kathryn Campbell

Nominating & Placement: Laura Dutton

Program Review: Tahnika Rodriguez

Sustainer Advisor: Johanna Heywood

Contributors

Cheers to the following people who spent countless hours contributing, preparing, and tasting recipes. And again, for contributing, preparing, and tasting even more recipes! Thanks to those who supported, coached, and encouraged us throughout this process. You have made our cookbook possible, and we hope that you are as pleased with this collection as we are. We also give our heartfelt thanks to those who have been inadvertently omitted.

Cortney Abney
Elaine Adams
Anna Adamson
Amber Lynn Alexander
Sherry Allison
Taylor Andersen
Betsy Anderson
Ann Andrews
Mary Arnold
Melanie Atchley
Pam Atherton
Libby Bailey
Angela Ballard
Carolyn Ballard
Hillary Barber
Anna Barnett
Julie Fleming Barringer
Keith Barry
Kimber Bastone
Molly Beard
Patsy Beatty
Caroline Bentley
Ouida Bianco
Caroline Bickel
Kelsey Bickley
Denna Biderman
Ginger Birnbaum
Barbara Blake
Pam Blanton

Sally Boals
Beth Botta
Autumn Witt Boyd
Rebecca Brinkley
Kathleen Brock
Jennie Brockman
Donna Brody
Nootsie Brooks
Carla Brown
Meredith Byrum Brown
Virginia Brown
Quincy Brunson
Brandi Buntain
Ashley Burnette
Graham Burns
Brittain Bussart
Maggie Butler
Kim Callaway
Carol Campbell
Elizabeth Campbell
Kathryn Campbell
Susan Campbell
Jennifer Canipe
Elizabeth Carriger
Martha Carriger
Wiki Carter
Nancy Caulkins
Amanda Cauthen
Sharon Chamberlain

Bettie Chester
Grace Clark
Shannon Clark
Christy Fazio Clegg
Susan Cobb
Elizabeth Collins
Julia Cook
Brandie Cookston
Priscilla Coon
Coughlin Cooper
Virginia Corey
Theresa Critchfield
Lele Crutchfield
Ann Currey
Susanna Darr
Ashley Davenport
Jessica Davenport
Leslie Davenport
Rebecca Davenport
Cristy DeBaby-Blanding
Stephanie Devine
Kali Ann DeWine
Anne Donnovin
Laura Dutton
Wendi Ehinger
Martha Elder
Karen Elliott
Missy Elliott
Brandi Engle

Contributors

Barbara Ensign
Ellen Epperson
Maggie Estes
Cynthia Fagan
Christy Falco
Ashley Farless
Elizabeth Farr
Connie Farrar
Dana Feldman
Margaret Ferguson
Sara Fields
Ashley Finch
Janet Fisher
Autumn Fitch
Kathryn Flanagan
Catherine Fore
Kami Fowler
Sarah Fowler
Jennifer Franklin
Marge Franklin
Crissy Furrow
Caroline Garner
Carolyn Rose Garner
Lucy Gates
Emily Geyer
Jill Glenn
Amanda Godin
Kathy Graham
Amy Gregory
Monica Griffin
Julie Guerry
Andee Guthrie

Ashley Guthrie
Annie Hagaman
Missy Hale
Annie Hall
Meredith Hamilton
Tracey Hankins
Chrissy Harris
Holley Hasting
Betsy Hawthorne
Barbara Helton
Joan Heywood
Johanna Heywood
Ellie Hill
Leah Hill
Melissa Hogue
Amy Holland
Katherine Holland
Leesa Jenkins Holliday
Ann Hon
Honor Hostetler
Lindsey Houston
Suzie Howick
Lauren Howley
Christina Humphrey
Meredith Ingle
Joy Irwin
Julie Irwin
Amy Jackson
Ronna-Renee Jackson
Kendall Jacobs
Lynn Jacobs
Laura Jennings

Chelsea Johnson
Kelly Johnson
Kellyann Johnson
Laura O'Kelley Johnson
Lee Johnson
Pam Johnson
Susan Johnson
Caroline Jones
Catherine Kain
Stacey Kaufmann
Megan Keen
Amanda Kelley
Kristen Kelly
Laura Ketcham
Susan Kirby
Natalie Kizziah
Jane Kline
Katie Koerner
Peggy Kovacevich
Peggy Laney
Mary (Teeny) Lassiter
Alice Lawwill
Kristin Leach
Karen Leavengood
Sheryl Leitner
Kacy Lemm
Lynda LeVan
M. J. Levine
Mary Stewart Lewis
Gina Liberto
Emily Lilley
Greta Lindsay

Contributors

Carey Long

Beth Lupton

Laurie Lynn

Brooke Maedel

AnnaLea Malone

Ashley Manning

Elizabeth Marr

Catherine Martin

Annan Matthews

Maria Matthews

Elizabeth McCallie

Maddin McCallie

Brooke McCants

Angela Lee McClister

Laura McDade

Leah McDaniel

Merrell McGinness

Shelley McGraw

Missy McKenna

Beth McKenzie

Sarah McKenzie

Becky McMahon

Carrie Meade

Dawn Meline

Anne Ford Melton

Elaine Merriman

Suzanne Mickles

Terry Miles-Adams

Alexia Miller

Melady Miller

Catherine Minor

Gina Mitch

Lauren Mitchell

Jennifer Mitts

Lindsey Monen

Taylor Monen

Emily Monroe

Diane Moore

Lesley Moore

Merry Madeline Moore

Tracy Moore

Katie Murchison

Barbara Murray

Kate Myers

Jennifer Nicely

Betsy Nichols

Liz Nichols

Chrissy Nolan

Suzanne Nolan

Teresa North

Robin Nunley

Andrea Odle

Cheryl Odom

Allison O'Neal

Margaret Overton

Courtney Paris

Sydni Paris

Kathy Patten

Pemmy Patten

Kristin Patterson

Nancy Petty

Anne Platt

Becky Pope

Sheila Porada

Laurel Powell

Caroline Prigmore

Miranda Pugh

Meghan Putnam

Laura Raby

Sally Ratterman

Debbie Red

Sara Page Red-Barnwell

Kelly Reese

Elizabeth Richards

Jean Richardson

Lindsay Richardson

Jasmin Rippon

Meredith Rivers

Melissa Robillard

Ginnie Robinson

Kathleen Robinson

Marty Robinson

Tahnika Rodriguez

Kate Rolen

Jill Rooks

Billie Rose

Margie Rowland

Simone Rudge

Michelle Ruest

Carly Russell

Kelsey Sabin

Kimberly Saldana

Ginny Sanders

Julia Suttles Saunders

Jennifer Schleger

Meg Scott

Contributors

Katey Seibels

Kara Serrano

Keeta Settle

Margaret Sexton

Virginia Anne Sharber

Abby Shipley

Melissa Shipp

Maggie Shutters

Shannon Silberman

Alison Skiles

Mallory Slaughter

Alison Smiley

Christine Smith

Gloria Murray Smith

Joyce Smith

Kate Smith

Heather Sneed

Starlet Speakman

Rhymes Stabler

Phyllis Steele

Estes Stephens

Carol Stephenson

Gloria Stewart

Jennifer Stone

Kitty Stone

Scottie Goodman Summerlin

Heather Sveadas

Rebecca Taylor

Niti Tejani

Katie Templeton

Amanda Terry

Amy Thomas

Marie Thornbury

Cassie Tindell

Leigh Todd

Molly Trainor

Emmie Treadwell

Abby Tucker

Karen Underwood

Courtney Valentine

Sanja Veledar

Carolyn Viens

Blair Waddell

Emily Walker

Jade Walker

Patsi Walker

Reagan Walker

Ann Walldorf

Flora Walldorf

Catherine Watjen

Taylor Watson

Dannis Weathersby

Whitney Webb

Dorris Wells

Robin Wheelock

Amanda Whitaker

Peggy White

Jennifer Williams

Jane Williamson

Carrie Willmore

Katie Wilson

Pamela Wilson

Susan Wilson

Lisa Winters

Charlotte Witry

Lindsay Wolford

Elizabeth Wood

Suzanne Wyche

Denyse Yingling

Theresa Youngquist

Bibliography

Allied Arts Chattanooga. "About Us." http://alliedartschattanooga.org/site/pages/about-us/overview.php (accessed July 20, 2010).

Battles for Chattanooga Museum, The. "About Us." http://www.battlesforchattanooga.com/open.html (accessed July 11, 2010).

Bluff View Art District. "History." http://www.bluffviewartdistrict.com/index.php (accessed July 18, 2010).

CanoeTennessee.com. "Canoeing The Tennessee River Blueway." http://canoetennessee.com/ (accessed July 29, 2010).

Chattanooga African American Museum. "About Us." http://www.caamhistory.org/ (accessed July 18, 2010).

Chattanooga Area Chamber of Commerce. "The Chattanooga Riverfront Story." http://www.chattanoogachamber.com/gettoknowus/riverfront.asp (accessed July 25, 2010).

_____. "Return to the River." http://www.chattanoogacando.org/newsandvideo/Trend_summer_04_pge10.asp (accessed July 25, 2010).

Chattanooga Area Convention and Visitors Bureau. *Chattanooga History and Trivia did you know?*. Chattanooga: Chattanooga Area Convention and Visitors Bureau.

_____. "Chattanooga Lookouts." http://www.chattanoogafun.com/media-room/media-kit/# (accessed July 20, 2010).

_____. "Chattanooga National Cemetery." www.chattanoogafun.com (accessed July 20, 2010).

_____. "Chattanooga Nature Center." http://www.chattanoogafun.com/media-room/media-kit/release.asp?id=148 (accessed July 29, 2010).

_____. "Chattanooga Symphony & Opera: The Region's Only Professional Orchestra." http://www.chattanoogafun.com/media-room/media-kit/ (accessed July 20, 2010).

_____. "Coolidge Park & Renaissance Park." http://www.chattanoogafun.com/media-room/media-kit/release.asp?id=144 (accessed July 29, 2010)

_____. "Outdoors." http://www.chattanoogafun.com/outdoors/ (accessed July 29, 2010).

_____. "Rock City Gardens." http://chattanoogafun.com/media-room/media-kit/release.asp?id=136 (accessed July 20, 2010).

_____. "Tennessee Riverwalk." http://www.chattanoogafun.com/media-room/media-kit/# (accessed July 20, 2010).

ChattanoogaHasFun.com. "Coolidge Park and Coolidge Park Carousel." http://www. chattanoogahasfun.com/local-guide/attraction-guide/coolidge-park-coolidge-park-carousel/ (accessed July 26, 2010).

Chattanooga Magazine. "To Market, to Market." March/April 2010.

Chattanooga Market, The. "About Us: Press Kit." http://www.chattanoogamarket.com/about/ press/ (accessed July 20, 2010).

Chattanooga Nature Center, The. "What to See." http://www.chattanooganaturecenter.org/ what-to-see/ (accessed July 29, 2010).

Chattanooga Traditional Jazz Festival. "Home." http://www.chattanoogajazzfestival.com/index. html (accessed July 11, 2010).

Chattanooga Zoo. "Animals and Exhibits." http://www.chattzoo.org/ (accessed July 11, 2010).

Choo Choo Partners, L.P. "Chattanooga Choo Choo." http://www.choochoo.com/ (accessed July 20, 2010).

City of Chattanooga. "Coolidge Park." http://www.chattanooga.gov/prac/30_1096.htm (accessed July 11, 2010).

_____. "Parks and Recreation." http://www.chattanooga.gov/PRAC/30_ DirectoryParkFacilities.htm (accessed July 11, 2010).

_____. "Tivoli Theatre." http://www.chattanooga.gov/EAC/2919_TivoliTheatre.htm (accessed July 20, 2010).

HELLOCHATTANOOGA.com. "Southern Belle Riverboat Company." http://www. hellochattanooga.com/Articles/Attraction/1274/Southern_Belle_Riverboat_see_the_sights_of_ Chattanooga_from_the_Tennessee_River.Cfm (accessed July 29, 2010).

Houston Museum of Decorative Arts. "The History of the Houston Museum." http://www. thehoustonmuseum.com/history.html (accessed July 26, 2010).

Hunter Museum of American Art. "About the Hunter." http://www.huntermuseum.org/about/ (accessed July 18, 2010).

MoonPie. "About." http://moonpie.com/about#1 (accessed July 29, 2010).

Nicely, Maury. *Chattanooga Walking Tour & Historic Guide.* Chattanooga: Stillhouse Hollow Press, 2005.

Bibliography

Nightfall Concert Series. "History." http://www.nightfallchattanooga.com/history.aspx (accessed July 11, 2010).

Northwest Georgia's Historic High Country. *Blue & Gray Trail, A Guide to The Civil War Sites in Northwest Georgia & Chattanooga.* Dalton: Northwest Georgia's Historic High Country, 2008.

Outdoor Chattanooga. "Air." http://www.outdoorchattanooga.com/376.htm (accessed July 11, 2010).

_____. "Land." http://www.outdoorchattanooga.com/378.htm (accessed July 11, 2010).

_____. "Water." http://www.outdoorchattanooga.com/379.htm (accessed July 11, 2010).

Riverbend Festival. "General Information." http://www.riverbendfestival.com/pages/general-information (accessed July 11, 2010).

Rock City Gardens. "Barn History." http://www.seerockcity.com/pages/Barn-History/ (accessed July 29, 2010).

Ruby Falls. www.rubyfalls.com (accessed July 20, 2010).

Southeast Tennessee Tourism Association. *Civil War Trails: Fighting for the Rails.* Chattanooga: Southeast Tennessee Tourism Association. (2008)

Southern Belle Chattanooga Riverboat Co. "Special Events." http://www.chattanoogariverboat.com/www/docs/5.html (accessed July 11, 2010).

Southside Chattanooga. "Stroll the Historic Southside." http://southsidechattanooga.org/ (accessed July 26, 2010).

Tennessee Aquarium. "About Us." http://www.tnaqua.org/AboutUs.aspx (accessed July 18, 2010).

_____. "Fishing for Aquarium Fun Facts." http://www.tnaqua.org/Newsroom/faqsfun.asp (accessed July 18, 2010).

Tennessee Valley Railroad Museum. "A Brief History of TVRM." www.tvrail.com (accessed July 20, 2010).

United States Department of Veteran Affairs. "Chattanooga National Cemetery." http://www.cem.va.gov/CEM/cems/nchp/chattanooga.asp (accessed July 20, 2010).

USDA Forest Service Ocoee Whitewater Center. "About Us." http://www.fs.fed.us/r8/ocoee/aboutUs.shtml (accessed July 29, 2010).

What's On When. "Pops on the River." http://www.whatsonwhen.com/sisp/index.htm?fx=event&event_id=157681 (accessed July 11, 2010).

Index

Index

Index

Index

Index

Index

Index

Photograph Index

This constitutes an extension of the copyright page.

Cover photograph by MaryMargaret Chambliss

Page 2 – left to right starting from top left row – Black-eyed peas, Surefire Sangria, Choo Choo Scenic Drive, Peaches (MaryMargaret Chambliss); Lula Lake Falls (Warren-McLelland Aerial Photography); Downtown Chattanooga Riverfront (Vincent Rizzo)

Page 3 – left to right starting from top left row – The W Road, Signal Mountain (Vincent Rizzo); Cannon at Point Park, Lookout Mountain, Sidewalk dance steps at North Shore (MaryMargaret Chambliss); Downtown Chattanooga and Lookout Mountain (Warren-McLelland Aerial Photography); Blackberries at the Chattanooga Market, Beans and peppers at the Chattanooga Market (Billie Rose); Cosmopolitan Punch, Downtown at 2nd and Broad, Lavender (MaryMargaret Chambliss); River Gorge (Warren-McLelland Aerial Photography); Best Biscuits (MaryMargaret Chambliss)

Page 11 – Rock City Barn (Vincent Rizzo)

Page 13 – Cherry blossom trees in bloom (iStockphoto®)

Page 15 – Pan-Seared Tarragon Chicken, Best Biscuits, Spring Peas (MaryMargaret Chambliss)

Page 29 – clockwise from top left – Legacy Tea, Crab-Stuffed Mushrooms, Porch Party Pasta Salad, bowl of eggs (MaryMargaret Chambliss)

Page 43 – River Queen Carrot Cake (iStockphoto®)

Page 53 – Picnic basket (Billie Rose)

Page 55 – Creamy Lemonade Pie (MaryMargaret Chambliss)

Page 67 – Yummy Breakfast Pastry (MaryMargaret Chambliss)

Page 81 – clockwise from top left – Figs in a Ribbon, BFT Sandwiches, Battles of Chattanooga, Fruited Mint Tea, Delta Queen of Chattanooga (MaryMargaret Chambliss)

Page 95 – Pumpkin (iStockphoto®)

Page 97 – Easy-Peasy Skillet Mac and Cheesy (MaryMargaret Chambliss)

Photograph Index

To order additional copies of

Seasoned to Taste

SAVORING THE SCENIC CITY
WITH THE JUNIOR LEAGUE OF CHATTANOOGA

Contact
The Junior League of Chattanooga
622 East 4th Street
Chattanooga, Tennessee 37403
www.jlchatt.org
423.267.5053